AN OUTLINE HISTORY OF

# Spanish American Literature

# AN OUTLINE HISTORY OF

# Spanish American Literature

PREPARED UNDER THE AUSPICES OF THE

Instituto Internacional de Literatura Iberoamericana

BY A COMMITTEE CONSISTING OF

## E. Herman Hespelt

CHAIRMAN AND EDITOR

Irving A. Leonard      John E. Englekirk

John T. Reid      John A. Crow

F. S. Crofts & Co.    1941    New York

# Preface

This *Outline History of Spanish American Literature* is the work of a committee appointed at the Ann Arbor Conference on Latin American Studies in the summer of 1939 for the purpose of studying the scope and subject matter of courses on Spanish American literature in the colleges and universities of the United States.

The committee was chosen to represent different sections of the country—the Northeast, the South, the Midwest, the Southwest, and the Pacific Coast—and its first project was to make a survey of the present status of such courses in representative institutions of these sections.

A questionnaire was prepared which inquired in detail into the aims, methods, and materials of the courses now being given and asked what changes the instructors in charge thought desirable. The response to the questionnaire was most generous. Not only did those colleagues to whom it was sent give of their time to answer the questions submitted to them. They also sent book lists, chronological tables, syllabi, and other aids which they had devised and prepared in working out their own courses. In all, answers were received from thirty institutions, large and small. In addition to the universities represented by the members of the committee these co-operating institutions were:

| INSTITUTION | PROFESSOR REPORTING |
|---|---|
| Barnard College | Carolina Marcial Dorado |
| Boston University | Samuel Waxman |
| Colgate University | Graydon S. DeLand |
| College of Wooster | Ruth Richardson |
| Dartmouth College | J. M. Arce |
| Harvard University | G. P. Rivera |
| Miami University | Willis K. Jones |

| INSTITUTION | PROFESSOR REPORTING |
|---|---|
| New Mexico Normal University | Antonio Rebolledo |
| Northwestern University | William Berrien |
| Stanford University | Juan B. Rael |
| University of Alabama | Marshall Nunn |
| University of Arizona | George R. Nichols |
| University of Cincinnati | Dillwyn F. Ratcliff |
| University of Colorado | Stuart Cuthbertson |
| University of Indiana | Agapito Rey |
| University of Iowa | E. K. Mapes |
| University of Missouri | J. Warshaw |
| University of New Mexico | Albert R. Lopes |
| University of North Carolina | Sturgis E. Leavitt |
| University of Redlands | Eva R. Price |
| University of Southern California | W. F. Rice |
| University of Texas | Nina L. Weisinger |
| University of Washington | G. W. Umphrey |
| University of Wisconsin | Eduardo Neale-Silva |
| Yale University | Frederick B. Luquiens |

The detailed results of the survey were reported to the Instituto Internacional de Literatura Iberoamericana at its 1940 meeting and will be published elsewhere. Some of the general conclusions to be drawn from the study, however, may be noted here since they have in large measure determined the scope and character of this outline.

In the first place it was obvious that, although there is a great diversity both in the material studied and in the methods of presentation obtaining in the various institutions, there is a certain uniformity in the external set-up of the course. Making allowances for numerous exceptions, it seems fair to say that the typical course in Spanish American literature in a North American college is two semesters in length, meets three times a week each semester, and is elected by upperclassmen after two years (or a "reading knowledge") of college Spanish.

The problem of selecting material which can profitably be presented to these students within the limits of such a course is a difficult one. It is the more difficult because much of the material in the earlier periods is relatively unavailable and because in the later periods there is no definitely established canon of required reading. It is the purpose of this outline to help the instructor make this selection and to indicate where the available materials may be found.

In the second place it was apparent from the survey that there are two distinct methods of approach to the study of literature. They might be called the deductive and the inductive approach. The instructor using the first method spends most of the time in the classroom lecturing or discussing the history and development of the literature, its social background, and the biographies and significance of outstanding authors. The actual reading of the works of literature is done outside of class. The instructor using the inductive approach, on the other hand, spends his time in the classroom reading and discussing the books themselves. The student gets his information concerning the historical development of the literature from reference books outside of class. The committee in preparing this outline has tried to keep in mind the needs of both groups. The present volume is essentially a topical outline of the history of Spanish American literature arranged by periods and genres with references under each topic to the leading handbooks and works of criticism [a large dot (•) marks those that are especially recommended] and suggestions as to the works of literature to be read in each period and the available editions of these works. At the same time, for those classes using the inductive method, it provides in the "Introductory Summary" to each section and in the sketches of the individual authors enough historical and biographical information to give the student some sense of the continuity of the development of the literature and of the relative value—intrinsic and historical—of the works he is reading.

The committee has wished to take a realistic attitude about the amount of work the student in a "typical" class can be expected to cover, but it has also wished to give—in so far as it was able—a fair and adequate account of the development of the literature of Spanish America. It has therefore included a great deal more material than the average student of the "typical" class can assimilate. Those authors whose works it considers absolutely essential for him to know are marked with a double asterisk (**) and those next in importance with a single asterisk (*). It is expected that the others will be read only by superior students or more advanced classes.

The outline has been divided into five sections corresponding to the five generally recognized periods of Spanish American literature. Each member of the committee is responsible for one section. The authors of the various sections are:

Section A, "The Colonial Period (1519–1808)," Irving A. Leonard, Brown University.

Section B, "The Period of Struggle for Independence (1808–1826)," John T. Reid, Duke University.

Section C, "The Nineteenth Century before Modernism (1826–1888)," E. Herman Hespelt, New York University.

Section D, "Modernism—Realism (1888–1910)," John A. Crow, University of California at Los Angeles.

Section E, "The Contemporary Period (1910–1941)," John E. Englekirk, Tulane University.

In spite of this divided authorship and in spite of differences in the problems presented by each period, an attempt has been made to keep the treatment of the sections as nearly uniform as possible. Some variations and inconsistencies have been unavoidable.

The committee wishes to express its grateful appreciation of the invaluable help it received from the colleagues who answered the questionnaire and to thank especially for their helpful suggestions and collaboration Professors J. M. Arce, William Berrien, who was a member of the original committee, E. K. Mapes, Antonio Rebolledo, J. Warshaw, and Marion Zeitlin, who supplied many of the titles included in the appended list of works of Brazilian literature.

E. H. H.

# Contents

Bibliography     xiii

Section A: The Colonial Period (1519–1808)     1

Section B: The Period of Struggle for Independence (1808–1826)     28

Section C: The Nineteenth Century before Modernism (1826–1888)     44

Section D: Modernism—Realism (1888–1910)     78

Section E: The Contemporary Period (1910–1941)     119

Appendix: A Bibliographical Introduction to Brazilian Literature for Those Reading Only English and Spanish     161

Index of Authors Mentioned in the Outline     167

# Maps

Explorations in Northern Spanish America     3

Explorations in Southern Spanish America     4

Principal Settlements in Colonial South America     9

Spanish America during the War for Independence     33

Mexico, Central America, and the Caribbean     51

South America Today     87

# Bibliography

The following works are referred to more than once in the course of this outline. For the sake of brevity only the name of the author (or editor) of these works is cited in the text unless two or more works of the same author have been used. In that case an abbreviated title is also quoted.

Works to which reference is made only once are cited in full immediately after the topic of which they treat.

Books published in Spain or Spanish America which are mentioned in this volume may be ordered from F. C. Feger, 70 Fifth Avenue, New York City, or from G. E. Stechert & Co., 31 East 10th Street, New York City.

## HISTORICAL BACKGROUND

Bryce, James, *South America: Observations and Impressions,* London and New York, Macmillan, 1912.

Chapman, Charles E., *Colonial Hispanic America: A History,* New York, Macmillan, 1933.

Chapman, Charles E., *Republican Hispanic America,* New York, Macmillan, 1937.

García Calderón, F., *Latin America: Its Rise and Progress,* London and New York, Scribner, 1913.

Kirkpatrick, F. A., *Latin America: A Brief History,* New York, Macmillan, 1939.

Rippy, J. Fred, *Historical Evolution of Hispanic America,* 2nd ed., New York, Crofts, 1940.

Shepherd, William R., *Latin America,* New York, Holt, 1914.

Ugarte, Manuel, *The Destiny of a Continent,* New York, Knopf, 1925.

Wilgus, A. Curtis (ed.), *Colonial Hispanic America,* Washington, D.C., The George Washington Univ. Press, 1936.

Wilgus, A. Curtis, *The Development of Hispanic America,* New York, Farrar and Rinehart, 1941.

Wilgus, A. Curtis (ed.), *Modern Hispanic America,* Washington, D.C., The George Washington Univ. Press, 1933.

Williams, Mary W., *People and Politics of Latin America,* Boston, Ginn, 1938.

## LITERARY HISTORY AND CRITICISM

Abreu Gómez, Ermilo, *Clásicos, románticos, modernos,* Mexico City, Botas, 1934.

Barrera, Isaac J., *Literatura ecuatoriana,* Quito, Ed. Ecuatoriana, 1939.

Barrera, Isaac J., *Literatura hispanoamericana,* Quito, Univ. Central, 1934.

Beltrán, Oscar R., *Manual de historia de la literatura hispanoamericana,* Buenos Aires, Manuel Tato, 1938.

*Bibliographies of Spanish-American Literature* prepared by the Harvard Council on Hispano-American Studies, 3 vols., Cambridge, Mass., Harvard Univ. Press, 1931–1935.

Blanco-Fombona, Rufino, *Grandes escritores de América,* Madrid, Renacimiento, 1917.

Blanco-Fombona, Rufino, *El modernismo y los poetas modernistas,* Madrid, Mundo Latino, 1929.

Carrión, Benjamín, *Los creadores de la nueva América,* Madrid, Soc. Gen. Esp. de Lib., 1928.

Cejador y Frauca, Julio, *Historia de la lengua y literatura castellana,* 14 vols. in 15, Madrid, Rev. de Arch., Bibl. y Museos, 1915–1922.

Chacón y Calvo, José M., *Ensayos de literatura cubana,* Madrid, Calleja, 1922.

Coester, Alfred, *A Literary History of Spanish America,* 2nd ed., New York, Macmillan, 1928.

Cometta Manzoni, Aida, *El indio en la poesía de América española,* Buenos Aires, Joaquín Torres, 1939.

[Crispo Acosta, Osvaldo] "Lauxar," *Motivos de crítica hispanoamericanos,* Montevideo, Mercurio, 1914.

[Díaz Arrieta, Hernán] "Alone," *Panorama de la literatura chilena durante el siglo XX,* Santiago, Nascimento, 1931.

Donoso, Armando, *La otra América,* Madrid, Calpe, 1925.

Englekirk, John E., *Poe in Hispanic Literature,* New York, Instituto de las Españas, 1934.

Estrella Gutiérrez, Fermín, and Suárez Calimano, Emilio, *Historia de la literatura americana y argentina,* Buenos Aires, Kapelusz & Cía, [1940].

García Calderón, Ventura, *Del romanticismo al modernismo,* Paris, Soc. de Ed. Literarias y Artísticas, 1910.

García Calderón, Ventura, *Semblanzas de América,* n.p., Ed. por la Rev. Hisp.-Am. "Cervantes," n.d. (Biblioteca Ariel).

García Godoy, F., *Americanismo literario,* Madrid, Ed. América, 1917.

García Godoy, F., *La literatura americana de nuestros días,* Madrid, Soc. Esp. de Lib., 1915.

García Velloso, E., *Historia de la literatura argentina,* 7th ed., Buenos Aires, Estrada, n.d.

Giorgi, M. V., *Curso de historia de la literatura hispano-americana,* Buenos Aires, Talleres Graf. "El Misionero," 1937.

Goldberg, Isaac, *Studies in Spanish American Literature,* New York, Brentano's, 1920.

González Peña, Carlos, *Historia de la literatura mexicana,* 2nd ed., México, Cultura y Polis, 1940.

Guzmán, Augusto, *Historia de la novela boliviana,* La Paz, Revista "México," 1938.

Holmes, Henry Alfred, *Martín Fierro, an Epic of the Argentine,* New York, Instituto de las Españas, 1923.

Iguíniz, Juan B., *Bibliografía de novelistas mexicanos,* México, Monografías bibliográficas mexicanas, 1926.

Jiménez Rueda, Julio, *Historia de la literatura mexicana,* México, Botas, 1934.

"Lauxar": see Crispo Acosta, Osvaldo.

Mapes, E. K., *L'influence française dans l'œuvre de Rubén Darío,* Paris, H. Champion, 1925.

Marinello, Juan, *Literatura hispanoamericana,* México, Ed. de la Univ. Nacional, 1937.

Meléndez, Concha, *La novela indianista en Hispanoamérica,* Madrid, Hernando, 1934.

Menéndez y Pelayo, Marcelino, *Antología de poetas hispanoamericanos.* (See under Anthologies.)

Meza Fuentes, Roberto, *De Díaz Mirón a Rubén Darío,* Santiago, Nascimento, 1940.

Miranda, Estela, *Poetisas de Chile y Uruguay,* Santiago, Nascimento, 1937.

Moses, Bernard, *The Intellectual Background of the Revolution in South America, 1810–1824,* New York, Hispanic Society, 1922.

Moses, Bernard, *Spanish Colonial Literature in South America, 1810–1824,* New York, Hispanic Society, 1922.

Northup, George T., *An Introduction to Spanish Literature,* Chicago, Univ. of Chicago Press, 1925.

Ortega, José J., *Historia de la literatura colombiana,* Bogotá, Cromos, 1935.

Picón–Salas, Mariano, *Formación y proceso de la literatura venezolana,* Caracas, Acosto, 1940.

Ratcliff, D. F., *Venezuelan Prose Fiction,* New York, Instituto de las Españas, 1933.

Read, J. Lloyd, *The Mexican Historical Novel, 1826–1910,* New York, Instituto de las Españas, 1939.

Rojas, Ricardo, *La literatura argentina,* 8 vols., Buenos Aires, Lib. "La Facultad," 1924–1925. ("Los gauchescos," 2 vols.; "Los coloniales," 2 vols.; "Los proscriptos," 2 vols.; "Los modernos," 2 vols.) (*Obras* de Ricardo Rojas, Vols. VIII–XV.)

Romera Navarro, M., *Historia de la literatura española,* Boston, Heath, 1928.

Sánchez, Luis Alberto, *Historia de la literatura americana,* 2nd ed., Santiago, Ercilla, 1940.

Sánchez, Luis Alberto, *Historia de la literatura peruana,* Lima, Imp. Euforión, 1921.

Sánchez, Luis Alberto, *La literatura del Perú,* Buenos Aires, Imp. de la Univ., 1939.

Sánchez, Luis Alberto, *La literatura peruana: Derrotero para una historia espiritual del Peru,* [Lima, 1929].

Santos González, C., *Poetas y críticos de América,* Paris, Garnier, 1913.

Silva Castro, Raúl, *Retratos literarios,* Santiago, Ercilla, 1932.

Solar Correa, E., *Semblanzas literarias de la colonia,* Santiago, Nascimento, 1933.

Spell, Jefferson Rea, *Rousseau in the Spanish World before 1833,* Austin, Univ. of Texas Press, 1938.

Torres-Ríoseco, Arturo, *Grandes novelistas de la América hispana: I, Los novelistas de la tierra,* Berkeley and Los Angeles, Univ. of California Press, 1941.

Torres-Ríoseco, Arturo, *La novela en la América hispana,* Berkeley, Univ. of California Press, 1939.

Torres-Ríoseco, Arturo, *Novelistas contemporáneos de América,* Santiago, Nascimento, 1940.

Torres-Ríoseco, Arturo, *Precursores del modernismo,* Madrid, Calpe, 1925.

Valdaspe, Tristán, *Historia de la literatura argentina e hispanoamericana,* Buenos Aires, Moly & Laserre, n.d.

Valera, Juan, *Cartas americanas,* [Madrid], n.d. (*Obras completas,* vols. 41–42).

Zum Felde, Alberto, *Crítica de la literatura uruguaya,* Montevideo, Maximino García, 1921.

Zum Felde, Alberto, *Proceso intelectual del Uruguay,* Montevideo, Imp. Nac. Colorada, 1930.

## ANTHOLOGIES

Barreda, E. M., *Nuestro parnaso,* Buenos Aires, J. L. Dassa, 1914.

Beltrán, Oscar R., *Antología de poetas y prosistas americanos,* 4 vols., Buenos Aires, Anaconda, [1937].

Beltroy, Manuel, *Las cien mejores poesías (líricas) peruanas,* Lima, Euforión, 1921.

Blackwell, Alice Stone, *Some Spanish-American Poets,* 2nd ed., Philadelphia, Univ. of Pennsylvania Press, 1937.

Castro Leal, Antonio, *Las cien mejores poesías (líricas) mejicanas,* México, Porrúa, 1935.

Coester, Alfred, *An Anthology of the Modernista Movement in Spanish America,* Boston, Ginn, [1924].

Coester, Alfred, *Cuentos de la América española,* Boston, Ginn, [1920].

Craig, G. Dundas, *The Modernist Trend in Spanish-American Poetry,* Berkeley, Univ. of California Press, 1934.

Crow, John A., *Cuentos hispánicos,* New York, Holt, 1939.

Dantín Cereceda, Juan, *Exploradores y conquistadores de las Indias occidentales, 1492–1540,* Madrid, Junta para Ampliación de Estudios, 1922 (Biblioteca literaria del estudiante, 17).

De Vitis, M. A., *A Spanish Reader for Beginners,* Boston, Allyn and Bacon, 1920.

Ford, J. D. M., *A Spanish Anthology,* New York, Silver Burdett, 1901.

Frank, Waldo (ed.), *Tales from the Argentine,* New York, Farrar and Rinehart, 1930.

García Calderón, Ventura, *Los mejores cuentos americanos,* Barcelona, Maucci, n.d.

García Calderón, Ventura (ed.), *Los místicos de Hojeda a Valdés,* Paris, 1938 (Biblioteca de cultura peruana, 7).

García Prada, Carlos, *Antología de líricos colombianos,* 2 vols., Bogotá, Imp. Nacional, 1936.

Heliodoro Valle, R., *La nueva poesía de América,* Mexico, 1924.

Henríquez Ureña, Pedro, and Borges, J. L., *Antología clásica de la literatura argentina,* Buenos Aires, A. Kapelusz, n.d.

Hills, E. C., *Bardos cubanos,* Boston, Heath, 1901.

Hills, E. C., *The Odes of Bello, Olmedo and Heredia,* New York and London, Putnam, 1920.

Hills, E. C., and Morley, S. G., *Modern Spanish Lyrics,* New York, Holt, [1913].

Holmes, Henry Alfred, *Spanish America in Song and Story,* New York, Holt, 1932.

Jiménez Rueda, Julio, *Antología de la prosa en México,* 2nd ed., México, Botas, 1938.

Kennedy, James, *Modern Poets and Poetry of Spain,* London, Longman, 1852.

Laguardia, C. G. B., and Laguardia, G. G. B., *Argentina: Legend and History,* New York, Sanborn, 1919.

Leavitt, Sturgis E., *Tres cuentos sud-americanos,* New York, Crofts, 1935.

Lillo, Samuel A., *Literatura chilena con una antología contemporánea,* 5th ed., Santiago, Nascimento, 1930.

Menéndez y Pelayo, Marcelino, *Antología de poetas hispanoamericanos,* 4 vols., Madrid, Tip. de la Rev. de Archivos, 1893–1895, reprinted 1927–1928.

Monterde, Francisco, *Antología de poetas y prosistas hispanoamericanos modernos,* México, Univ. Nacional, 1931.

Noé, Julio, *Antología de la poesía argentina moderna (1896–1930) con notas biográficas y bibliográficas,* 2nd ed., Buenos Aires, "El Ateneo," 1932.

Onís, Federico de, *Antología de la poesía española e hispanoamericana (1882–1932),* Madrid, Hernando, 1934.

Oyuela, Calixto, *Antología poética hispanoamericana,* 3 tomos en 5 vols., Buenos Aires, Angel Estrada y Cía, 1919–1920.

Pagano, José L., *El parnaso argentino,* 9th ed., Barcelona, Maucci, n.d.

*Poemas clásicos: La cautiva, El Fausto, Santos Vega,* Buenos Aires, Colección Claridad, n.d.

*Poetas gauchescos: Hidalgo, Ascasubi, Del Campo,* introducción por E. F. Tiscornia, Buenos Aires, Losada, [1940] (Colección de textos literarios).

Poor, A. B., *Pan-American Poems,* Boston, The Gorham Press, 1918.

Porras Barrenechea, Raúl, *Pequeña antología de Lima (1535–1935),* Madrid,
1935.

Puig, Juan de la C., *Antología de poetas argentinos,* Buenos Aires, M. Biedma,
1910.

Romera Navarro, M., *Antología de la literatura española,* Boston, Heath, 1933.

Rosenberg, S. L. Millard, and Templin, Ernest H., *A Brief Anthology of
Mexican Prose,* Stanford University, California, Stanford Univ. Press, 1928.

Rosenberg, S. L. Millard, and Templin, Ernest H., *A Brief Anthology of Mexican Verse,* Stanford University, California, Stanford Univ. Press, 1928.

Santos González, C., *Antología de poetas modernistas americanos con un ensayo
acerca del modernismo en América por R. Blanco-Fombona,* Paris, 1913.

Solar Correa, E., *Poetas de Hispanoamérica,* Santiago, Cervantes, 1926.

Starr, Frederick, *Readings from Modern Mexican Authors,* Chicago, Open Court
Publ. Co., 1904.

Torres-Ríoseco, Arturo, *Antología de la literatura hispanoamericana,* 2nd ed.,
New York, Crofts, 1941.

Torres-Ríoseco, Arturo, and Kress, Margaret K., *Chilean Short Stories,* New
York, Prentice-Hall, 1929.

Torres-Ríoseco, Arturo, and Sims, E. R., *Mexican Short Stories,* New York,
Prentice-Hall, 1932.

Underwood, E. W., *Anthology of Mexican Poets,* Portland, Maine, The Mosher
Press, 1932.

Walsh, Thomas, *The Catholic Anthology,* New York, Macmillan, 1928.

Walsh, Thomas, *Hispanic Anthology: Poems Translated from the Spanish by
English and North American Poets,* New York and London, Putnam, 1920.

Weisinger, Nina Lee, *Readings from Spanish-American Authors,* Boston, Heath,
[1929].

Wilkins, Lawrence A., *Antología de cuentos americanos,* with a critical introduction by Federico de Onís, Boston, Heath, [1924].

## OTHER WORKS OF GENERAL REFERENCE

Arjona, Doris King, and Arjona, Jaime Homero, *A Bibliography of Textbooks of Spanish Published in the United States (1795–1939)*, Ann Arbor, Michigan, Edwards Brothers, 1939.

Grismer, Raymond L., *A Reference Index to Twelve Thousand Spanish American Authors*, New York, Wilson, 1939.

Hanke, Lewis (ed.), *Handbook of Latin American Studies*, 5 vols., Cambridge, Harvard Univ. Press, 1935–1940.

Martin, Percy Alvin, *Who's Who in Latin America*, Stanford University, California, Stanford Univ. Press, [1940].

AN OUTLINE HISTORY OF

# Spanish American Literature

# The Colonial Period (1519–1808)

## BY IRVING A. LEONARD

## INTRODUCTORY SUMMARY

There is a certain aptness in considering the colonial period, taken as a whole, as the Middle Ages of Spanish America, and its literature as essentially medieval. Feudal institutions in Spain were beginning to disintegrate at the time of the conquest, but this process had not advanced sufficiently to prevent the transference to the newly acquired provinces of a fundamentally medieval civilization with the predominance of the Church in temporal affairs and of theology in intellectual life. The existence of a large, subjugated population of sedentary Indians in the richest areas of the New World was bound to perpetuate a social and economic order which was breaking up in Europe; the vast numbers of serfs at the disposal of Spanish overlords rendered such a society practically inevitable. With necessary local modifications, then, the mode of life and thought of the Middle Ages in Europe was re-established in the new communities organized by the Spaniards and survived far beyond the chronological period of the Middle Ages elsewhere. In such a conservative order, rigidly controlled by a medieval Church and by representatives of a distant Crown, literature was cultivated mainly as an aristocratic privilege or, more often, as a means of promoting the work of that Church and of glorifying it as an institution. Under these circumstances colonial letters could only develop as a somewhat stunted branch of Spanish literature; hence the bulk of the literary production of the colonies consists of sermons, religious guides, missionary chronicles, theological tracts, and, later, an almost uninterrupted flood of gongoristic verse, reflecting the current bad literary taste. Some exceptional figures and works, however, mark the progress of three centuries of colonial cultural life.

Colonial literature of the early sixteenth century was the product of much the same influences as those at work in the mother country and was directly conditioned by them. In Spain the bare, medieval chronicle was giving way to the more luxuriant form of the Renaissance, and the prodigious exploits of the conquerors and the vast new world whose exotic wonders they revealed served as a powerful stimulant to the newer style of detailed, descriptive histories. Such records and chronicles as those of Hernán Cortés, Bernal Díaz del Castillo, Bartolomé de las Casas, Toribio de Benavente, and Pedro Cieza de León are literary monuments of permanent value and are not devoid of novelistic elements to interest the reader.

Also in the Spain of this glorious period of high adventure the Italian influences in narrative verse were keenly felt, and a whole school of epic poets, men of action in the New World, inspired by the stirring models of Ariosto and Tasso, sprang into being. The metrical compositions of this group reflected the zestful spirit of their time and record, sometimes in immortal verse, the incredible feats of valor of the conquistador and the legends of his Indian opponents. The work of Ercilla, the poet of action as well as words, best epitomizes this heroic genre, for the realism and descriptive vigor of his *La araucana* are never quite equaled in the diminuendo of similar but less inspired poems during the century following. Nevertheless, these later rhymed narratives also reveal the enthusiasm and love of action which characterized the first exuberant decades of Spain in the New World and have left a literary legacy which can still be enjoyed. Indeed, their success, and later that of versified plays, was so great that both tended to discourage the use of prose as a medium of creative expression during the whole colonial period.

By the beginning of the seventeenth century the era of tremendous expansion was at an end. The weakened motherland was obliged to content herself with consolidating gains already made and with thrusting forward here and there a defensive frontier against foes, foreign and domestic. With the passing of the conquistador a settled state of society

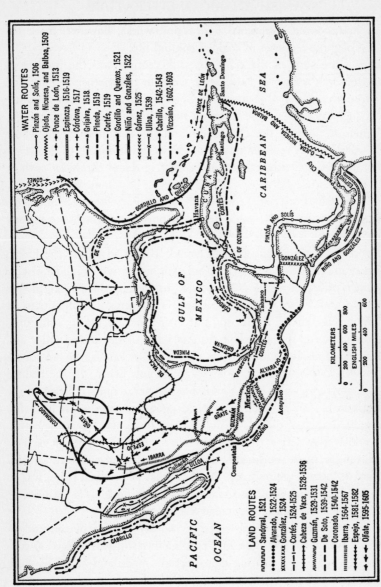

EXPLORATIONS IN NORTHERN SPANISH AMERICA

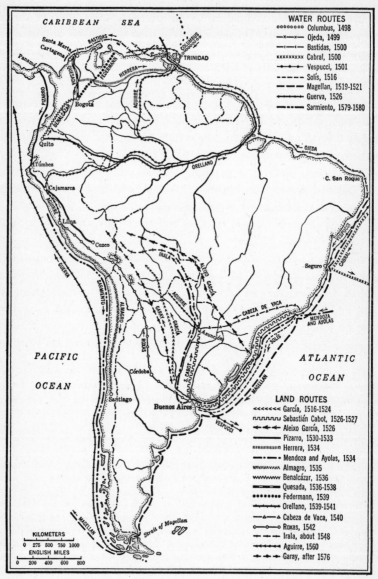

WATER ROUTES
ooooooo Columbus, 1498
—x—x— Ojeda, 1499
—¡—¡— Bastidas, 1500
xxxxxxxxx Cabral, 1500
—•—•—• Vespucci, 1501
— — — Solís, 1516
— — — Magellan, 1519-1521
←—→—→ Guerva, 1526
———— Sarmiento, 1579-1580

LAND ROUTES
<<<<<< García, 1516-1524
nnnnnn Sebastián Cabot, 1526-1527
—←—←— Aleixo García, 1526
———— Pizarro, 1530-1533
muuuuuu Herrera, 1534
—•—•— Mendoza and Ayolas, 1534
vvvvvvvv Almagro, 1535
wwwwww Benalcázar, 1536
━━━━━ Quesada, 1536-1538
•••••••• Federmann, 1539
↤↤↤↤↤ Orellano, 1539-1541
——△—△ Cabeza de Vaca, 1540
o——o——o Roxas, 1542
—←—←— Irala, about 1548
←←←←← Aguirre, 1560
—←—←— Garay, after 1576

CARIBBEAN SEA

PACIFIC OCEAN

ATLANTIC OCEAN

Santa Marta
Cartagena
Panamá
Bogotá
Quito
Túmbez
Cajamarca
Lima
Cuzco
Córdoba
Santiago
Buenos Aires
Asunción
Seguro
C. San Roque
TRINIDAD
Strait of Magellan

KILOMETERS
0  275  500  750  1000
ENGLISH MILES
0  200  400  600  800

EXPLORATIONS IN SOUTHERN SPANISH AMERICA

gradually emerged, accompanied by an increasing cultivation of the arts and social refinements. Universities were soon established almost simultaneously in Mexico City and Lima,[1] and these, with other educational institutions founded later, began to flourish in the seventeenth century. About them as a nucleus grew a small but increasing leisure class [2] with varying degrees of interest in intellectual pursuits. Their eyes, however, were turned toward the motherland for inspiration, and it was her models they sought to imitate, neglecting the materials so richly at hand in their own environment.

There is no dearth of important works of erudition and imagination from colonial presses [3] during the last two centuries of Spanish rule, but they are far outnumbered in the continuous deluge of verse which accompanied them. Some poetry possessed merit, but too often it degenerated into mere verbal gymnastics. No occasion, seemingly, was too insignificant to commemorate with such effusions, so that births, marriages, deaths in the royal and viceroyal families, and particularly the arrival of a new viceroy to take office, as well as the more frequent religious and secular festivals, were all signals for an outburst in print of more or less poetic rhapsody. The custom of celebrating "certámenes," or poetical contests, and, later, the various literary academies were pro-

[1] The Royal and Pontifical University of Mexico was chartered in 1551 and opened in 1553; the University of San Marcos de Lima was also chartered in 1551 but did not open until about 1576. The Spaniards established some twenty-one universities in addition to these two. See John T. Lanning, *Academic Culture in the Spanish Colonies* (Oxford University Press, London, New York, Toronto, 1940), pp. 14, 23.

[2] A number of outstanding poets and writers of Spain made extended visits to the colonies, particularly during the first century after the conquest. Some of these were Gutierre de Cetina (1520–1557), Juan de la Cueva (1550–1609), and Mateo Alemán (1547–1614). Francisco de Borja (Prince of Esquilache), who was the viceroy of Peru from 1615 to 1621, is said to have held a celebrated literary salon in his palace in Lima.

[3] Printing presses were established in the Spanish colonies as follows: Mexico City, 1535; Lima, 1584; Puebla de los Ángeles (Mexico), 1640; Guatemala, 1660; Paraguay Jesuit Missions, 1700; Havana (Cuba), 1707; Oaxaca (Mexico), 1720; Bogotá, 1738; Ambato (Ecuador), 1754; Quito, 1760; Córdoba (Argentina), 1766; Cartagena (Colombia), 1769; Santiago de Chile, 1776; Buenos Aires, 1780; Santo Domingo, 1782; Guadalajara (Mexico), 1793; Veracruz (Mexico), 1794. See José Torre Revello, *Orígenes de la imprenta en España y su desarrollo en la América Española* (Buenos Aires, 1940).

ductive of much bad verse, too much of which has been preserved to posterity.

All this activity might have resulted in the production of more worthy verse if the colonies had not imitated so sedulously the literary decadence and vices of the mother country. Unfortunately, all these defects were faithfully reproduced and exaggerated in the intellectual centers of Spain's ultramarine possessions. The innovations of Don Luis de Góngora y Argote (1561–1627), the Cordovan bard, inspired an army of untalented imitators, and the curse of Gongorism, with its ridiculous conceits, distorted syntax, affected style heavily freighted with classical and mythological allusions, numbing Latinisms, and other marks of pedantry, descended upon colonial literature, prose as well as verse, with blighting effect. The contagion of such excessively bad taste spread even to that inspired genius, Sor Juana Inés de la Cruz. Nearly every writer succumbed to this devastating plague, including sober-minded intellectuals, many of whose works otherwise command respect, such as Sigüenza y Góngora of the University of Mexico and especially Peralta Barnuevo of the University of San Marcos at Lima, the author of the ponderous epic *Lima fundada*. It was indeed the triumph of form over idea, and little of the literature of the time conveys any message for today.

The literary habits of the seventeenth carried well into the following century, but the influence of French letters and ideas was early felt, much earlier than is usually acknowledged. The accession of the Bourbons in 1700 to the Spanish throne was instrumental in opening colonial ports to French ships, which brought French styles, customs, and literature into the overseas realms, particularly the viceroyalty of Peru, almost as soon as into Spain itself. One of the earliest adaptations in the Spanish language of Corneille's tragedies was made by Peralta Barnuevo and performed in Lima about 1720, and the accompanying dramatic skits clearly betray the influence of Molière, Boursault, and Scarron. As the eighteenth century advanced, more and more French works were introduced and read, at first freely and openly, later more surreptitiously as the revolutionary doctrines of rationalistic philosophers alarmed the reactionary

Spanish authorities and moved them to attempt through the Inquisition and other agencies to exclude such literature from the colonies. But printed French plays, essays, tracts, and pamphlets circulated clandestinely and, together with the numerous literary and scientific societies springing up in the last decades of the century, served as a freshening breeze blowing through the scholasticism and pedantry of colonial intellectual life. A wave of interest in systematic investigation and scientific thought began to spread, and the new critical spirit manifested itself in the appearance of periodicals which, though they flourished all too briefly, afforded evidence that the medieval culture implanted nearly three centuries before was crumbling. With the distant, rumbling thunder of the approaching wars of independence growing more audible, a new epoch in Spanish American letters was at hand.

General References: Barrera, *Lit. hisp.,* 7–192. Beltrán, *Manual,* Chap. I. Coester, *Lit. Hist.,* Chap. I. Estrella Gutiérrez and Suárez Calimano, Chap. I. Moses, *Span. Col. Lit., passim.* Sánchez, *Hist. de la lit. am.,* 46–150.

I. Historical background.

    1. The extent of Spanish conquests and explorations in the New World.

        a. Aztec capital, later called Mexico City, taken by Cortés in 1521 with subjugation of neighboring regions quickly following. Northern explorations of Núñez Cabeza de Vaca, Hernando de Soto, and Vásquez de Coronado.

        b. Pizarro, after executing Atahualpa, entered Cuzco, Peru, capital of the Inca empire, in 1533. He founded Lima in 1535.

        c. Gonzalo Jiménez de Quesada in 1536 climbed to the high plateau of New Granada to conquer Chibcha Indians, and founded Santa Fe de Bogotá, capital of present-day Colombia, in 1538.

    **d.** Pedro de Valdivia crossed deserts of northern Chile in 1540, founding the city of Santiago de Nueva Estremadura the following year, and was killed in war with Araucanian Indians in 1554.

2. The organization of the Spanish empire in the New World.

    **a.** House of Trade established at Seville in 1503 to control trade, navigation, and emigration to colonies. Council of Indies established in Spain by king in 1524 for political administration of colonies.

    **b.** Viceroyalties. Large territorial units administered by personal representative of the king, i. e., viceroy. Viceroyalty of New Spain (Mexico) established in 1535; of Peru, in 1544; of New Granada (northern South America), in 1718, abolished in 1723, and re-established in 1739; of Río de la Plata (Argentina, Uruguay, Paraguay, and Bolivia), in 1776.

    **c.** Captaincies-General. Usually frontier subdivisions headed by royal officers with civil and military powers, as Guatemala (1527) and Chile (about 1600).

    **d.** *Audiencias.* Territorial and judicial subdivisions of a viceroyalty presided over by *oidores* with judicial, administrative, and advisory powers. Number of *audiencias* increased to thirteen important ones in eighteenth century.

3. Colonial society.

    **a.** Whites: Peninsulars, or Spaniards born in Spain; Creoles, or colonials born in America of Spanish or European parentage; small element of non-Spanish Europeans.

    **b.** Negroes: slaves, agricultural laborers, and domestic servants.

    **c.** Indians: sedentary and semicivilized; nomadic and wild.

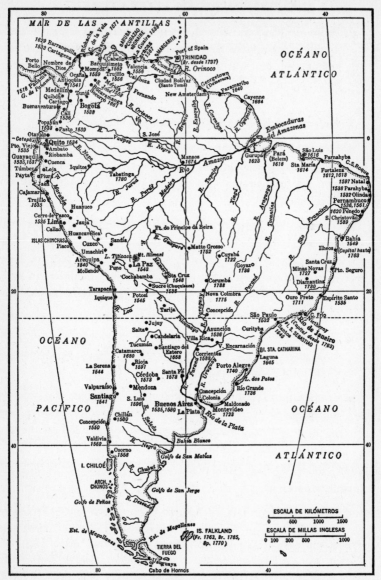

PRINCIPAL SETTLEMENTS IN COLONIAL SOUTH AMERICA

**d.** Mixed races: basic mixtures: mestizo (white and Indian); mulatto (Negro and white); and *zambo* or *zambaigo* (Indian and Negro).

**4.** Culture and education in the Spanish American colonies.

**a.** Predominance of medieval Church and theology.

**b.** Scholastic universities, *colegios,* and seminaries.

References: Chapman, *Col. Hisp. Am.,* Chaps. III–IV, VII–IX, XI. García Calderón, F., Chap. II. Kirkpatrick, Chaps. III–IV. Rippy, Chaps. IV–VI. Shepherd, Chaps. II–VI. Wilgus, *Development,* Chaps. IV–X, XII–XIII. Williams, Chaps. IV–X.

**II.** Important factors influencing literature during the colonial period.

**1.** Influences of Peninsular literature at the time of the Conquest and later.

**a.** The new spirit in writing history.
References: •Northup, Chaps. VI, XI. Read, 1–28. •Sánchez, *Hist. de la lit. am.,* Chap. III.

**b.** Narrative poetry.
References: Cometta Manzoni, 28–120. Sánchez, *Hist. de la lit. am.,* Chap. IV. •Sánchez, *Hist. de la lit. per.,* Chap. I.

**2.** Colonial society and cultural life.
References: Barreda Laos, Felipe, *La vida intelectual del Virreinato del Perú,* 2d ed., Buenos Aires, 1937. •Jones, Cecil K., "The Transmission and Diffusion of Culture in the Spanish American Colonies," Wilgus, *Col. Hisp. Am.,* Chap. X. •Lanning, John Tate, *Academic Culture in the Spanish Colonies,* New York, 1940. •Leonard, Irving A., "Colonial Society," Wilgus, *Col. Hisp. Am.,* Chap. IX. Williams, Chaps. IX, X.

3. Gongorism in America.

REFERENCES: González Peña, Part II, Chaps. I–II. •Leonard, Irving A., "Some Curiosities of Spanish Colonial Poetry," *Hispania*, XV (1932), 39–54. Pirotto, Armando D., *La literatura en América: El coloniaje*, Montevideo, 1937, 151–166. •Sánchez, Luis Alberto, *Góngora en América*, Quito, 1927. Sánchez, *Hist. de la lit. am.*, 83–102. •Sánchez, *Hist. de la lit. per.*, Chaps. VIII–IX. Sánchez, *Lit. per.: Derrotero*, II, Chap. V. Schons, Dorothy, "The Influence of Góngora on Mexican Literature during the Seventeenth Century," *Hispanic Review*, VII (1939), 22–34.

4. French influences and scientific ideas.

REFERENCES: Jiménez Rueda, *Historia*, Chap. VII. •Moses, *Span. Col. Lit.*, Chaps. XVI–XVII. Sánchez, *Hist. de la lit. am.*, Chap. VII. Sánchez, *Lit. per.: Derrotero*, II, Chap. VI. •Sánchez, *Lit. per.*, Chap. III. Spell, Chap. VII.

## III. The chroniclers.

1. Of the conquest and exploration.

**     a. (MEXICO) **Hernán Cortés** (1485–1547). The conqueror of Mexico was born in Medellín, Extremadura, in Spain, and spent two years as an indifferent student at the University of Salamanca. Eager for adventure, he sailed to Santo Domingo in 1504, later joining Diego Velásquez in the conquest of Cuba, where Cortés became a planter. He took advantage of the expedition of Governor Velásquez to the mainland to undertake the conquest of Mexico. During the years 1519–1526 Cortés sent five famous dispatches, called *cartas relaciones*, to Charles V of Spain. These terse, vivid reports possess literary merits comparable to the *Commentaries* of Julius Caesar and to the *Anabasis* of Xenophon. Cortés died a broken and disappointed man near Seville at the age of 62.

SUGGESTED READING: Selections from the *Cartas relaciones.*

TEXTS: *Despatches from Mexico to Charles V* (ed. Day), New York, American Book Co., 1933. Romera Navarro, *Antología,* 163–166, letter of October 30, 1520. Dantín Cereceda, 145–175, selections from first, second, fourth, and fifth dispatches. Jiménez Rueda, *Antología,* "Prisión de Moctezuma y explotación de minas," 31–42.

EDITION: *Cartas de relación de la conquista de Méjico,* 2 vols. in 1, Madrid, 1922.

CRITICAL REFERENCES AND TRANSLATIONS: Gayangos, Pascual de (trans.), *The Fifth Letter of Hernan Cortes to the Emperor Charles V,* Hakluyt Society Publications, vol. 40, London, 1868. MacNutt, Francis A., *Letters of Cortes,* 2 vols., New York, Putnam, 1908; English translation with notes and biographical introduction. Morris, J. Bayard (ed. and trans.): Hernando Cortés, *Five Letters,* New York, Robert M. McBride and Co., 1929.

*   b. (MEXICO) **Bernal Díaz del Castillo** (1492–1584). The soldier-historian was born in Medina del Campo, Spain, and came to America in 1514 with Pedro Árias Dávila, Governor of Darien. Shortly thereafter Bernal Díaz went to Cuba and was a member of the Grijalva expedition along the Yucatan coast in 1518. Casting his lot with Cortés, he took part in 119 battles during the conquest of Mexico and was rewarded with an allotment of Indians or "encomienda" in Guatemala, where he remained most of the rest of his long life. Disagreeing with the account of López de Gómara in the latter's *Crónica de la conquista de la Nueva España* (1552), the doughty soldier of Cortés wrote his *Verdadera historia de la conquista de la Nueva España* in vigorous, unpolished style. This narrative, distinguished for its sincerity and remarkable detail, was not published until 1632, nearly a half century after the death of its author.

SUGGESTED READING: "Recibimiento que les hizo Moctezuma a los conquistadores."

TEXTS: Jiménez Rueda, *Antología,* 43–52. Dantín Cereceda, short selections, 121–129, 134–141.

EDITION: Ramírez Cabañas, Joaquín (ed.): Bernal Díaz del Castillo, *Historia verdadera de la conquista de la Nueva España,* 3 vols., Mexico City, Pedro Robredo, 1939.

CRITICAL REFERENCES AND TRANSLATIONS: Cunninghame Graham, R. B., *Bernal Díaz del Castillo,* London, 1915. Keatinge, Maurice (trans.): Bernal Díaz del Castillo, *The True History of the Conquest of Mexico,* New York, Robert M. McBride and Co., 1938. •Maudslay, Alfred P. (trans.): Bernal Díaz del Castillo, *The True History of the Conquest of New Spain,* 5 vols., Hakluyt Society Publications, London, 1908–1916; with copious notes, maps, plans, and bibliographical information. Stephens, Kate, *The Mastering of Mexico,* New York, Macmillan, 1916; an abridgment of Bernal Díaz del Castillo's *True History,* based principally on the translation of John Ingram Lockhart.

c. (MEXICO AND PARAGUAY) **Álvar Núñez Cabeza de Vaca** (1490?–1564?). Regarding the author of the curious memoirs of an extraordinary and terrible Odyssey through the south and southwest of the United States and north of Mexico entitled *Naufragios* few biographical facts are known. He appears to have been a native of Seville, Spain, grandson of the conqueror of the Canary Islands; coming to the Indies, he joined the ill-fated expedition of Pánfilo de Narváez to Florida. His hardships resulting from this disaster are vividly related in the *Naufragios.* Years later he was appointed "adelantado" and governor of La Plata and explored the rivers of Argentina and Paraguay. Pero Hernández recorded these later adventures in a book called *Comentarios.*

TEXT: Dantín Cereceda, brief selections, 295–300.

EDITION: *Naufragios y comentarios, con dos cartas,* Madrid, Calpe, 1922.

CRITICAL REFERENCES: Bishop, Morris, *The Odyssey of Cabeza de Vaca,* New York, 1933; a general account of Cabeza de Vaca's wanderings. Hodge, Frederick W. (ed.), "The Narrative of Álvar Núñez Cabeza de Vaca," *Spanish Explorers in the Southern United States, 1528–1543,* New York, Scribner, 1907, 19–52. •Rojas, Ricardo, "Los coloniales," 144–165.

2. Ecclesiastical chroniclers.

**Bartolomé de las Casas** (1475–1566). The so-called "Apostle of the Indies," born in Seville, Spain, went to Santo Domingo as a layman and later to Cuba. Profoundly distressed by the cruelties which the Indians suffered at the hands of his countrymen, Las Casas joined the Dominican order and dedicated his life to laboring for the protection of the new wards of the Crown from exploitation by the Spaniards. His excessive zeal moved him to exaggerate conditions which he described in his writings, notably his celebrated *Brevísima relación de la destruición de las Indias;* these exercised a profound influence on opinion abroad in his own time and upon posterity. Las Casas became Bishop of Chiapa and made numerous voyages back and forth across the Atlantic in his struggles in behalf of the Indians. Death overtook him in Spain after a long life while he was still gallantly fighting for his cause.

TEXT: Dantín Cereceda, selections, 9–11, 64–69, 74–78, 82–85, 289–295.

EDITION: Serrano y Sanz, M. (ed.), *Historiadores de Indias,* Vol. I, Madrid, 1909 (Nueva biblioteca de autores españoles, 13).

CRITICAL REFERENCES: Brion, Marcel, *Bartolomé de las Casas,* New York, 1929, Chap. IX. Manakee, H. R., "Las Casas, Father of the Indians," *Catholic World,* 135, 561–572.

3. Native chroniclers.

** (PERU) **Inca Garcilaso de la Vega** (1539–1615) was born in
Cuzco, Peru, of a Spanish father, cousin of the great Spanish poet
of the same name (1501?–1536), and of an Incan princess, cousin
of Atahualpa, whom Pizarro executed. At the age of twenty the
young mestizo went to Spain in a vain effort to obtain an inher-
itance to which he was entitled through his father. In 1564 he
enlisted in the Spanish army and rose to the rank of captain.
Much of the remainder of his life was spent in Córdova, where
he lies buried. Besides an excellent translation of León Hebreo's
*Diálogos de amor,* he wrote three important historical works
which have won him a secure place in the annals of Spanish
American letters. These are *La Florida del Inca, o la historia del
Adelantado Hernando de Soto,* the more highly esteemed *Los
comentarios reales que tratan del origen de los Incas,* and the *Historia general del Perú.*

SUGGESTED READING:  Selections from *Comentarios reales.*

TEXTS: *El reino de los Incas* (ed. Bardin), Boston, Allyn and
Bacon, 1918, 21–29, 64–78, 96–104. *Páginas escogidas* (ed. García
Calderón), Paris, 1938 (Biblioteca de cultura peruana); contains
selections from eight books of the *Comentarios reales* and from
*La Florida del Inca,* preceded by an excellent study of the Inca
Garcilaso by José de la Riva Agüero (pp. 13–49) and a bibli-
ography.

CRITICAL REFERENCES AND TRANSLATIONS: Fitzmaurice-Kelly,
Julia, *El Inca Garcilasso de la Vega,* London, Oxford University
Press, 1921.   Markham, Clements R.: *Garcilaso de la Vega, First
Part of the Royal Commentaries,* 2 vols., Hakluyt Society Publications (Vols. XLI, XLV), London, 1869–1871; translation with
notes and introduction. Rojas, Ricardo, "Los coloniales," 306–
326. Sánchez, *Lit. per.: Derrotero,* II, Chap. II.

**IV.** The poets.

1. Epic.

**\*\***    **a.** (CHILE) **Alonso de Ercilla** (1533–1594) was born in Madrid. He became a favorite of Philip II of Spain and accompanied this monarch in 1554 to England, where Ercilla met the newly appointed "adelantado" of Chile, Gerónimo de Alderete, and became interested in the New World. With royal permission Ercilla reached Lima, Peru, in 1556, and then proceeded to Chile, where he fought as a captain in the army of García Hurtado de Mendoza against hardy, warlike Araucanian Indians. In the midst of campaigning he wrote parts of the great epic poem *La araucana,* later completed upon his return to Spain. The first part appeared in 1569, and the second and third parts were printed in 1578 and 1589 respectively. After further travels in Europe Ercilla married and settled in Madrid, where he spent the remainder of his life.

SUGGESTED READING:   Selections from *La araucana.*

TEXTS: Holmes, *Span. Am.,* 141–143. Lillo, 12–13. Romera-Navarro, *Antología,* 150–156. Torres-Ríoseco, *Antología,* 141–143. Weisinger, 28–42.

EDITION: Huntington, Archer M. (ed.): Alonso de Ercilla, *La araucana,* New York, 1902; facsimile of the first and second parts.

TRANSLATION: Walsh, *Hisp. Anth.,* 221–225.

CRITICAL REFERENCES: Menéndez y Pelayo, IV, v–xiv. •Moses, *Span. Col. Lit.,* Chap. V. Solar Correa, 11–48.

**b.** (CHILE) **Pedro de Oña** (1570–1643?). Born in Valdivia, Chile, the son of a Spanish captain fighting Indians in southern Chile, Oña is the first native Chilean to achieve distinction in literature and is generally considered the foremost poet of that country in the colonial period. He attended the University of

San Marcos in Lima, Peru, 1590–1592, and then took part in an expedition sent to put down an insurrection in Quito, Ecuador. In 1596 he published the first part of his *Arauco domado,* inspired by Ercilla's epic; it reveals less merit than its model but demonstrates Oña's skill as a versifier in an original octave verse form. Other poems are: *Ignacio de Cantabria* (1639), a pious work celebrating Loyola, founder of the Jesuit order; *Temblor de Lima en 1609; Río Lima al río Tibre;* and *El vasauro,* an epic poem of eleven cantos, which appeared in print for the first time in its entirety in 1941.

SUGGESTED READING: *Arauco domado,* Canto V.

TEXTS: Lillo, 19–23 (excerpt). Menéndez y Pelayo, IV, 5–29. Oyuela, I, 4–34.

EDITION: Medina, José T. (ed.): Pedro de Oña, *Arauco domado,* edición crítica de la academia chilena, Santiago de Chile, 1917.

CRITICAL REFERENCES: •Moses, *Span. Col. Lit.,* 189–197. Solar Correa, 51–98.

c. (MEXICO) **Bernardo de Balbuena** (1562–1627), one of the best descriptive poets of the whole colonial period, is identified with Mexico, though born in Valdepeñas, Spain. Arriving in Mexico as a child, he early displayed precocious literary talent. Joining the church, he served in a number of parishes, beginning about 1592, later becoming abbot in Jamaica. During a sojourn of some four years in Spain he became a doctor of theology in the University of Sigüenza. In 1620 he was appointed Bishop of Puerto Rico, during which episcopate his palace was sacked by the Dutch. Two years later he died in San Juan. Three important works are associated with his name: *La grandeza mexicana,* a long descriptive poem of Mexico City in the last years of the sixteenth century, first printed in 1604; *El siglo de oro en las selvas de Erifile,* a collection of eclogues (1608); and *Bernardo, o victoria de Roncesvalles* (1624), a vast poem of five thousand octaves dealing with the legend of Bernardo del Carpio.

SUGGESTED READING: Selections from *La grandeza mexicana*.

EDITIONS: Van Horne, John (ed.): Bernardo de Balbuena, *La grandeza mexicana,* Urbana, University of Illinois, 1930; a critical edition with extensive notes and introduction. Van Horne, John (ed.), *"El Bernardo" of Bernardo de Balbuena,* Urbana, University of Illinois, 1927; a critical edition.

CRITICAL REFERENCES: Menéndez y Pelayo, I, xlvi–lvi; includes textual fragments of Balbuena's poems. •Van Horne, John, *Bernardo de Balbuena: Biografía y crítica,* Guadalajara, Mexico, Imprenta Font, 1940.

**d.** (PERU) **Diego de Ojeda (Hojeda)** (1571?–1615). Few facts are known of the life of this poet, who was born in Seville, Spain, and who as a youth came to Peru, where he joined the Dominican order in 1591. He served as prior in a convent in Cuzco and later in Huánuco de los Caballeros, where he died. A gifted poet, to him belongs the distinction of writing what is considered the best sacred epic in the Spanish language. His *Cristiada,* composed in a convent of Lima and published in 1611, deals with the life of the Savior and may conceivably be likened to Milton's *Paradise Lost.* Though marred by diffuseness and theological disquisitions, it contains numerous passages of great beauty.

SUGGESTED READING: Selections from *La cristiada*.

TEXT: García Calderón, *Los místicos;* contains selections from Books VI, VIII, XI, XII of *La cristiada.*

EDITION: Corcoran, Sister Mary Helen Patricia (ed.), *La cristiada de fray Diego de Hojeda,* Washington, Catholic University, 1935; a critical edition, with notes and introduction.

CRITICAL REFERENCES: Menéndez y Pelayo, III, clxxxv–clxxxviii. Sánchez, *Hist. de la lit. per.,* Chap. VI.

**2.** Lyric and satiric.

** **a.** (Mexico) **Sor Juana Inés de la Cruz** (1651–1695). The greatest lyric poet and feminist of the colonial period was Juana Inés de Asbaje y Ramírez de Cantillana, the name by which she was known before she took the veil as a nun. Born in San Miguel de Nepantla, Mexico, she was a child of exceptional precocity, learning to read when three years old. Studying everything within her reach, she astonished the learned professors of the University of Mexico by her knowledge. A maid of the viceroy's wife, she took religious vows at the age of sixteen, giving herself wholly to a life of seclusion, surrounded by her books. She wrote many poems and even plays of a sacred nature, occasionally rising high above the literary abuses and gongoristic habits of her time. Her death occurred in Mexico City during an epidemic when she was forty-four years old.

Suggested Reading: "Redondillas contra las injusticias de los hombres al hablar de las mujeres." "Redondillas en que describe racionalmente los efectos irracionales del amor." "Romance en que expresa los efectos del amor divino." Sonnets "Retrato" and "Detente sombra de mi bien esquivo."

Texts: Beltrán, *Antología,* I, 20–27. Castro Leal, 16–25. Jiménez Rueda, *Antología,* 103–110, "Respuesta a Sor Filotea de la Cruz." *Los empeños de una casa* (ed. Jiménez Rueda), Mexico City, 1940 (Biblioteca del estudiante universitario, 14). Menéndez y Pelayo, I, 5–59. Oyuela, I, 99–133. Rosenberg and Templin, *Verse,* 5–12. *Obras escogidas,* Buenos Aires, Mexico City, Espasa-Calpe, 1939 (Colección austral, 12). Torres-Ríoseco, *Antología,* 144–145. *Sonetos* (ed. Villaurrutia), Mexico City, 1941. Weisinger, 45–54; includes prose selections.

Edition: Abreu Gómez, Ermilo (ed.): Sor Juana Inés de la Cruz, *Poesías,* edición, prólogo y notas, Mexico City, Botas, 1940 (Clásicos de México, I).

TRANSLATIONS: Blackwell, 148–153. Malone, John, "The Mexican Nun: La monja de México: Juana Yñes [*sic*] de la Cruz (1651–1695)," Charles D. Warner (ed.), *Library of the World's Best Literature*, New York, J. A. Hill and Co., 1896–1898, Vol. XVII, 9936–9964. Underwood, 219–223. Walsh, *Hisp. Anth.*, 357–362. Walsh, *Cath. Anth.*, 214–216.

CRITICAL REFERENCES: •Abreu Gómez, Ermilo, *Clásicos, románticos, modernos*, Mexico City, Botas, 1934, 57–84. Chávez, Ezequiel A., *Ensayo de psicología de Sor Juana Inés de la Cruz*, Barcelona, 1931. González Peña, 87–92. Lee, Muna, "A Charming Mexican Lady," *American Mercury*, IV (1925), 105–108. Menéndez y Pelayo, I, lxvi–lxxiv. •Nervo, Amado, *Juana de Asbaje*, Madrid, 1910 (*Obras completas*, VIII).

GENERAL BIBLIOGRAPHIES: Abreu Gómez, Ermilo, *Sor Juana Inés de la Cruz: Bibliografía y biblioteca*, Mexico City, 1934 (Monografías bibliográficas mexicanas, 29). Schons, Dorothy, *Bibliografía de Sor Juana Inés de la Cruz*, Mexico City, 1927 (Monografías bibliográficas mexicanas, 7).

\* **b.** (PERU) **Juan del Valle y Caviedes** (1652–1695?). A satiric poet of Peru famed particularly for his mordant wit and barbed attacks on medical quacks. Recently discovered documents indicate that, though most of his life was passed in Lima, he was born in the town of Porcuna, Andalusia, Spain. It is thought that he also spent a brief period in Spain when about the age of twenty. Few other facts are known of his life except that he kept a little shop in Lima and employed his leisure in writing poetry, which, because of its biting satire, irony, and blunt language, offers a sharp contrast to the artificial expression prevailing in contemporary literature. Many of these writings circulated in manuscript, and their robust humor won their author considerable renown. Under the title *Diente de Parnaso* many of these were later collected and published long after the poet's death. His *Poesías diversas,* another collection,

are less satiric and more conventional in theme, though treated
in unaffected language.

SUGGESTED READING: Selections from *Diente de Parnaso.*

TEXTS: Beltroy, 33–37. García Calderón, Ventura (ed.), *El
apogeo de la literatura colonial,* Paris, 1938 (Biblioteca de
cultura peruana, 5); numerous selections, pp. 202–271. García
Calderón, *Los místicos;* there is a devout sonnet of Caviedes
given on p. 183. Porras Barrenechea; "El poeta de la Ribera"
of Ventura García Calderón, on pp. 176–183, includes quotations from Caviedes' verse.

CRITICAL REFERENCES: Menéndez y Pelayo, III, ccx–ccxiii.
Sánchez, *Hist. de la lit. per.,* Chap. X.

c. (PERU) **Esteban de Terralla y Landa** (last half of eighteenth
century). Little is known of the life of this bitter satirist, who
wrote much verse under the pen name "Simón Ayanque." A
Spaniard by birth, he came to Peru in 1787 after a number of
years in Mexico and worked as an official in the mines. In
Lima he led a disorderly life and, becoming embittered with
the society of the viceregal capital, mercilessly flayed many of
its members and customs in a well-known poem entitled "Lima
por dentro y fuera" which gained notoriety more for its subject matter than for its merit. Other poems include a mock
will and testament after the manner of the great Spanish satirist Quevedo (1580–1645). Terralla also wrote panegyrical prose
works in the exaggerated style of the time, but these are de-
servedly forgotten.

TEXTS: García Calderón, Ventura (ed.), *Costumbristas y
satíricos: De Terralla a Yerovi,* Paris, 1938 (Biblioteca de cultura peruana, 9); includes selections from "Lima por dentro
y fuera," "Testamento cerrado," and "Testamento, codocilo,
última voluntad," 19–57. Porras Barrenechea, 238–244, gives
some "romances" by Terralla.

CRITICAL REFERENCES: Menéndez y Pelayo, III, ccxxxii–ccxxxv. ●Palma, Ricardo, *Apéndice a mis últimas tradiciones peruanas,* Barcelona, 1910; the chapter "El poeta de las adivinanzas" (pp. 281–311) gives a sketch of Terralla with numerous quotations from his poems, including the "Testamento"; Palma stresses Terralla's skill in composing riddles. Sánchez, *Hist. de la lit. per.,* 293–296; brief discussion with text of hitherto unknown sonnet.

**V.** Prose with novelistic elements.

No true novel appeared from colonial presses during the entire period of Spanish control despite the importation and relatively free circulation of this type of literature in the viceroyalties. Numerous works purporting to be historical or biographical nonfiction do, however, contain novelistic elements, and in them may be found the seeds of the Spanish American novel.

1. (MEXICO) **Carlos de Sigüenza y Góngora** (1645–1700). Born in Mexico City of Spanish and Creole parentage, he was the foremost intellectual figure and humanist of colonial Mexico, having distinguished himself as a poet, philosopher, historian, antiquarian, mathematician, and astronomer. Educated as a Jesuit, he early left the Order, subsequently becoming a professor of mathematics in the University of Mexico and chaplain of the Hospital del Amor de Dios, where he lived most of his adult life. An intimate friend of Sor Juana Inés de la Cruz, he wrote poetry but lacked her genius, struggling vainly against the affected fashion set loose by his illustrious relative, Don Luis de Góngora. Though his best contributions were in the field of science and history, his most readable works today are those in which, as a court chronicler of the viceroy, the Count of Galve, he reported contemporary events. His *Infortunios de Alonso Ramírez,* a biographical narrative of the misadventures of a Puerto Rican, is regarded by some critics as one of the beginnings of the Mexican novel. Sigüenza's scientific work brought

him in 1693 to Pensacola, Florida, which he surveyed and mapped. Death overtook him at the age of 55.

SUGGESTED READING: Selections from *Infortunios de Alonso Ramírez.*

TEXTS: Jiménez Rueda, *Antología,* 89–102, "De los franceses en América" and "Del ataque a la ciudad de Santiago de los Caballeros." *Relaciones históricas* (ed. Romero de Terreros), Mexico City, 1940 (Biblioteca del estudiante universitario, 13); contains modernized text of *Infortunios de Alonso Ramírez, Relación de lo sucedido a la armada de Barlovento,* and *Alboroto y motín de México del 8 de Junio de 1692.* Rosenberg and Templin, *Prose,* 16–19, "La madre Tomasina."

CRITICAL REFERENCES: Abreu Gómez, 13–55. González Peña, 104–106. •Leonard, Irving A., *Don Carlos de Sigüenza, a Mexican Savant of the XVII century,* Berkeley, California, 1929; discussion of *Infortunios of Alonso Ramírez* on pp. 29–36; also Chap. VI. Leonard, Irving A., and E. Abreu Gómez, *Carlos de Sigüenza: Poemas;* a study of Sigüenza's poetry with text of his collected verse.

2. (PERU) **Calixto Bustamente Carlos Inga, "Concolorcorvo"** (second half of eighteenth century). The identity of this writer is still undetermined. In his book *El lazarillo de ciegos caminantes* he calls himself Calixto Bustamente Carlos Inga and claims to have been the son of an Incan princess of Cuzco, where two sisters were, at the time of writing, nuns in a convent. His alias "Concolorcorvo" derives from his dark complexion as a mestizo. His book, which purports to have been published in Gijón in 1773, describes a journey made in company with a postal commissioner across the Argentine pampas and the Andes to Lima, and was written in a brisk, ironic, and witty style reminiscent of the Spanish satirist Quevedo. It offers vivid descriptions of contemporary scenes and customs in realistic language, affording a striking con-

trast to prevailing literary fashions. It is one of the most readable products of the literature of the colonial period.

SUGGESTED READING: *El lazarillo de ciegos caminantes,* Chap. I, II, or VIII.

TEXT: *El lazarillo de ciegos caminantes* (ed. García Calderón), Paris, 1938 (Biblioteca de cultura peruana, 6); gives entire text with preliminary note and bibliography by the editor.

EDITION: Leguizamón, Martiniano (ed.): Concolorcorvo, *El lazarillo de ciegos caminantes desde Buenos Aires hasta Lima,* Buenos Aires, 1908 (Biblioteca de la junta de historia y numismática americana, IV); with biographical and bibliographical notes by the editor.

CRITICAL REFERENCE: Moses, *Span. Col. Lit.,* 525–530.

**VI.** The colonial theater.

Only fragmentary evidence is preserved of considerable activity during the colonial period. Many plays by colonial dramatists were written, performed, but lost as they remained in manuscript. Only a few are known by title, and still fewer have survived in manuscript or printed form. In the sixteenth century drama served mainly the didactic purposes of the Church; in the seventeenth and eighteenth centuries works of Spanish dramatists were popular and were constantly played in the "corrales" or theaters of the larger cities. Special plays were written and performed for the more courtly or aristocratic circles of the viceroyalties, and a few of these are preserved. These closely imitated models of Spain and Europe both in theme and in treatment.

**1.** (MEXICO) **Fernán González de Eslava** (1534?–1601?), a Spaniard born probably in the vicinity of Seville, came to Mexico about 1559. Little further is known of his life, though he appears to have gained considerable renown in his lifetime. In 1610, years after his death, sixteen "coloquios" and an "entremés" from his pen were published. Though similar to "autos sacramentales," they are remarkable for their natural dialogue, simple plot, and comic touches. Characters that are not allegorical are often well drawn and natural. The theological lessons which they were designed to convey are set forth in simple and readily comprehensible language.

Texts: Rojas Garcidueñas, José (ed.), *Autos y coloquios del siglo XVI,* Mexico City, 1939 (Biblioteca del estudiante universitario, 4); includes "Coloquio de los cuatro Doctores de la Iglesia" and "Coloquio del Conde de la Coruña." Rojas Garcidueñas, José, *El teatro de Nueva España en el siglo XVI,* Mexico City, 1935; the appendix includes the text of Coloquio V ("De los siete fuertes"), an "entremés," and Coloquio XIV ("De la pestilencia").

Edition: *Coloquios espirituales y sacramentales y poesías sagradas* (ed. García Icazbalceta), Mexico City, 1877.

Critical References: Alonso, Amado, "Biografía de Fernán González de Eslava," *Revista de filología hispánica,* II (1940), 213–321. González Peña, 65–66. •Rojas Garcidueñas, *El teatro de Nueva España,* Chap. VI.

2. (Mexico) **Sor Juana Inés de la Cruz.** See Section A, IV, 2, a.

3. (Peru) **Pedro de Peralta Barnuevo** (1663–1743), the most remarkably versatile Creole of colonial Peru, was renowned as historian, jurist, theologian, mathematician, engineer, astronomer, poet, and dramatist, and was familiar with eight languages, in several of which he composed poems. He was born of Spanish and Creole parentage in Lima, where he spent his entire life. His extant published writings as a whole glaringly reveal the gongoristic, inflated style of writing of his time, to which he succumbed completely. Probably the most readable of his works today are his plays, particularly the shorter pieces which accompanied his three "comedias," *Triunfos de amor y poder,* a mythological play, *Afectos vencen finezas,* a Calderonian "comedia," and *Rodoguna,* a

recasting of Corneille's tragedy *Rodogune*. The last-mentioned and some of the shorter pieces represent the earliest French influences in Spanish American literature. Peralta's "entremeses" and "bailes" are comic and "costumbrista" in character, preserving popular speech and customs of early eighteenth-century Peru.

SUGGESTED READING: "Fin de fiesta" of *Afectos vencen finezas* or "Entremés" of *La Rodoguna*.

TEXTS: Beltroy, 63, sonnet, "En la muerte del virrey Castel-dos-rius." García Calderón, *Los místicos;* includes excerpts from prose work *Pasión y triunfo de Cristo* and "Romance delante de una imagen de Cristo crucificado."

EDITION: Leonard, Irving A. (ed.), *Obras dramáticas de Pedro de Peralta Barnuevo,* Santiago de Chile, 1937; with introduction on life and works.

CRITICAL REFERENCES: •Leonard, Irving A., "A Great Savant of Colonial Peru, Don Pedro de Peralta," *Philological Quarterly,* XVII (1933), 54-72. Menéndez y Pelayo, III, ccxxii–ccxxxi.

4. **Ollanta(y),** a Peruvian play originally written in Quechua verse, is the most important literary work composed in any indigenous American language and is famous more for its supposed composition before the conquest of Peru by the Spaniards than for its intrinsic merit. The play, whose action is situated in Cuzco, the Incan capital, deals with the love of Ollanta(y), a chieftain of lowly birth, and the princess Cusi-Coyllu, daughter of the Inca Pachacutic. This drama in the Quechua dialect came to light between 1770 and 1780 when a parish priest, Dr. Antonio Valdés, had the play performed before an Incan chieftain, José Gabriel Condorcanqui (1744–1781). The spirit of the play and its dramatic arrangement and versification indicate that it was composed in the eighteenth century on the model of the Spanish "comedia," and probably by Valdés, the priest of Tinta. It has subsequently been translated into various European languages.

TEXT IN SPANISH: Basadre, Jorge (ed.), *Literatura inca,* Paris, 1938 (Biblioteca de cultura peruana, 1); gives text together with some related studies.

ENGLISH TRANSLATION: Markham, Clements R., *Ollanta, an Ancient Ynca Drama,* translated from the original Quechua, London, 1871; contains Quechua text with an English translation.

CRITICAL REFERENCES: •Hills, E. C., "The Quechua Drama *Ollanta," Hispanic Studies* (Stanford Univ. Press, California, 1929), 47–105; one of the best studies made on the subject, originally published in *Romanic Review,* II (1911), 127–176. Rojas, Ricardo, *Un titán de los Andes,* Buenos Aires, Lozada, 1939; sums up author's investigations of the development of the legend of Ollanta(y) from earliest times in connection with his own dramatization of the subject.

# The Period of Struggle for Independence (1808–1826)

BY JOHN T. REID

## INTRODUCTORY SUMMARY

Social or political revolution and good literature are seldom congenial bedfellows. This truism accounts in part for the fact that literature in Spanish America during the wars of independence is interesting largely as an illustrative document of the Revolution itself. The men who penned the patriotic odes or composed the journalistic essays—the typical productions of the period—generally wrote, not as professional literary men, but as patriots who wielded the pen and the sword for a single purpose. The natural result was an improvised literature, brilliant with occasional sparks of passionate inspiration, but lacking the originality and polish of letters composed in more tranquil times. Likewise, we may seek in vain for restraint and subtlety. Poems forged in the glow of battle are not likely to be models of careful workmanship and delicacy.

It must not be thought, however, that the literature of this period represents the popular voice of the rough and ready soldier of the New World armies. The independence of the colonies did not mean in any real sense a social revolution. The leaders of the movement were, for the most part, Creole aristocrats, whose background and education were not essentially different from those of the Spanish masters whom they fought. The poets who sang the Revolution had been educated in the colonial universities and carried in their heads or their books all the classical lore which those universities so generously dispensed. It was perfectly natural, then, that their literary productions should be designed according to colonial specifications. The abundance of classical allusions, the bombastic grandilo-

28

quence, the opulent complexity of syntax—all these are characteristics which the revolutionary poets inherited from their colonial training. Even their patriotic fervor, which contrasts with the somnolence of the colonial intellectual life, was to some extent a reflection of the neoclassical patriotic poets of Spain, such as Gallego and Quintana.

In spite of this, the revolutionary literature is not colonial literature. Fresh breezes from France blew inspiration into the old forms. The political and literary ideas of Rousseau, however imperfectly understood and superficially assimilated, found their way into the colonies during the last years of the eighteenth century and helped to provide an ideological background for the independence movement and its literary manifestations. The ideals of freedom and democracy, based on the theory of the inalienable rights of man, furnished the slogans and war cries of the wars of independence, even though they were seldom translated into governmental realities.

Two social institutions of the revolting colonies were of peculiar importance in the stimulation of revolutionary literature and propaganda. During the last days of the colonial regime, periodicals began to spring up in Buenos Aires, Lima, Bogotá, and Mexico. Descendants of these journals provided a pulpit for many of the revolutionary polemists. Moreno and Monteagudo in the *Gaceta de Buenos Aires,* Nariño in *La bagatela,* and Fernández de Lizardi in *El pensador mexicano* made important contributions to the earnest, impassioned prose of the struggle for independence. During the period printing presses multiplied, often surreptitiously, with amazing rapidity. Presses were established in quick succession in Caracas, Guayaquil, Santiago, Angostura (Chile), Arequipa, Cuzco, Panama, and Trujillo. From them flowed pamphlets, tracts, and periodicals to carry the inflaming new gospel to all corners of the New World in revolt. Another institution of late colonial days, the literary society, flourished with political aims during the revolutionary years. Many of the fiery patriotic poems of the epoch were first read in the intimacy of these clubs. Perhaps the most notable of them was the famous Sociedad Patriótica Literaria of Buenos Aires.

It was inevitable that in the prose and especially in the verse of these writers one of the dominant notes should be a violent hatred of the Spaniard. In their eyes the Spaniards were cruel, tyrannical despots, and the revolutionary hymns are peppered with such phrases as "vil invasor," "tigres sangrientos," and "el déspota insolente." It was also inevitable that the Spanish American patriots should evoke, at least for literary purposes, the conquered glories of the Inca and Aztec civilizations. In their hatred of the conquistador and their efforts to improvise a natively American ideal, they glorified the noble Indian who had been crushed under the Spanish boot. It is important to note that men like Olmedo, who called upon the Inca Huayna Capac to witness the victories of the emancipating armies, actually knew little of the millions of Indians who lived in the nascent republics and probably cared less. The Incas for him and for many a lesser poet were merely a romanticized legend which suggested a convenient patriotic catchword. However, the interest in the Indian stimulated during these years undoubtedly influenced later movements which sought to interpret the Indian's place in American life.

Most of the poetry and prose of this period is a product, as we have indicated, of the educated, aristocratic classes. It is probable that the mestizos and the Indians who were the cannon fodder of the Revolution also had their martial literature—popular ballads and "coplas." We know that this was true in Argentina, where samples of such poetry have been preserved. They are lacking, of course, in the literary pomp of the cultured verse and show, as a refreshing contrast, colloquial language and a vigorous, folklore spirit.

As might be expected, few of the scores of revolutionary writers have achieved anything approaching lasting literary fame. José Joaquín Olmedo, Andrés Bello, and José María Heredia are the outstanding figures among the poets of the period, and Fernández de Lizardi is the only prose writer who rose above the limitations of the immediate political situation. Many others, to be sure, are still praised and revered by Spanish Americans as symbols of their freedom. They are representative figures, interesting to us as spokesmen of an amazing and significant epic.

General References: Barrera, *Lit. hisp.,* 193–276. Beltrán, *Manual,* Chap. II. Coester, *Lit. Hist.,* Chaps. II and III. Estrella Gutiérrez and Suárez Calimano, Chap. II. Moses, *Intel. Back.* Oyuela, I, 479–489. Sánchez, *Hist. de la lit. am.,* 151–200. Valdaspe, Chaps. II and III.

I. The background of political and military events.

1. The causes of the revolution: economic restrictions of Spanish colonial policy; growth of American spirit among Creoles and desire for political recognition; example of the revolt of North American colonies; spread of ideas of French Revolution. Immediate causes: English attack on Buenos Aires (1806, 1807); Napoleonic invasion of Spain (1807–1808).

2. San Martín and the campaigns in the south.
   Provisional junta established in Buenos Aires (1810).
   Belgrano's disastrous expedition against Upper Peru (1813).
   Declaration of Argentine independence (1816).
   San Martín's army defeats Spaniards, Chacabuco and Maipú, Chile (1817).
   Occupation of Lima (1821).
   Conference with Bolívar (1822).

3. Bolívar and the revolution in the north.
   Miranda's abortive revolt (1806).
   Declaration of independence, Caracas (1811).
   Temporary collapse of revolution (1812).
   Bolívar calls Congress of Angostura (1818).
   Defeats Spaniards, Boyacá, Colombia (1819), and Carabobo, Venezuela (1821).
   Emancipation of Ecuador (1822).
   Decisive defeat of Spain's armies in Peru, Ayacucho (1824).

4. Hidalgo and Mexico.
   Hidalgo's revolt (1810).

Morelos' victories and declaration of independence (1813).

Execution of Morelos (1815).

Conservative counterrevolt under Iturbide (1820–1821).

Iturbide, emperor of Mexico (1822).

His abdication after revolt of Santa Ana (1823) and theoretical establishment of constitutional government.

REFERENCES: Chapman, *Col. Hisp. Am.,* Chaps. XIII–XV. •García Calderón, F., Chap. III. Kirkpatrick, Chaps. VI–VIII. Rippy, 133–164. Shepherd, Chap. VII. •Williams, Chap. XIII.

II. Important factors influencing literature during the revolutionary period.

1. The introduction of French political and literary ideas, especially those of Rousseau.

REFERENCES: García Calderón, F., 81–85. •Spell, Chap. XIV.

(COLOMBIA) **Antonio Nariño** (1765–1823) as an example.

REFERENCES: •Mancini, Jules, *Bolívar y la emancipación de las colonias españolas desde los orígenes hasta 1815,* Paris, Bouret, 1923, 78–88. Otero Muñoz, Gustavo, *Semblanzas colombianas,* Bogotá, Ed. ABC, 1938, I, 138–152. Ortega, 60–67.

2. The flourishing of political journals and literary-political societies.

REFERENCES: •Gutiérrez, Juan María, "La sociedad literaria y sus obras," *Crítica y narraciones,* Buenos Aires, El Ateneo, 1928, 147–196. Ibarguren, Carlos, *Las sociedades literarias y la revolución argentina,* Buenos Aires, Espasa-Calpe, 1937. Moses, *Intel. Back.,* Chaps. V and VI. Rojas, "Los proscriptos," 165–175.

3. The revolutionary theater in Buenos Aires.

REFERENCES: •Beltrán, Oscar R., *Los orígenes del teatro argentino,* Buenos Aires, Luján, 1934, 59–84. García Velloso, 200–212.

Showing approximately the
Political Divisions in 1808
⊙ Capitals    ✕ Battlefields

MANHATTAN DRAFTING CO., INC., N.Y.

SPANISH AMERICA DURING THE WAR FOR INDEPENDENCE

**III.** Patriotic poetry of the Revolution.

1. General characteristics: grandiloquence, lack of restraint, classical allusions.

    REFERENCES: Gutiérrez, *op. cit.,* 121–146.  Rojas, "Los coloniales," 887–894.

2. "Indianismo" in patriotic poetry.

    REFERENCES: •Cometta Manzoni, 136–147.  Meléndez, 61–64. Rojas, "Los coloniales," 938–944.

3. The influence of the Spanish patriotic poets Quintana and Gallego.

    REFERENCE: Romera-Navarro, *Historia,* 459–463.

4. Outstanding poets.

   ** **a.** (ECUADOR) **José Joaquín Olmedo** (1790–1847) was born in Guayaquil and received a typical classical education in the University of San Marcos in Lima. This classical background is obvious in his poetry. His first original poem, "Silva a la muerte de María Antonia de Borbón" (1807), is the usual laudatory verse of the colonial epoch. When the independence movement began (1810), he was sent to Spain to represent his natal city in the Cortes of Cádiz. Later he held governmental positions in America. At Bolívar's request he composed his best-known poem, commemorating the Liberator's triumph at Junín. So pleased was Bolívar that he sent Olmedo to London on a special mission. When Ecuador became a republic (1830), he was elected its first vice-president. Held in high esteem by his countrymen, he died at the age of 67.

    SUGGESTED READING: "La victoria de Junín: Canto a Bolívar" (1825).

    TEXTS: Beltrán, *Antología,* I, 44–51 (abridged).  Hills, *Odes,*

45–82. Hills and Morley, 193–198 (abridged). Holmes, *Span. Am.*, 330–332 (abridged). Menéndez y Pelayo, III, 272–297. Monterde, 202–226. Oyuela, I, 205–236. Solar Correa, 17–25 (abridged). Valdaspe, 244–245 (abridged).

EDITION: *Poesías* ..., con notas, documentos y apuntes biográficos por Clemente Ballén, Paris, Garnier, 1896.

TRANSLATION: Poor, 53–58.

CRITICAL REFERENCES: Barrera, *Lit. ecuat.*, 109–117. Barrera, *Lit. hisp.*, 210–237. Beltrán, *Manual,* 82–91. Giorgi, 88–91. Menéndez y Pelayo, III, cix–cxli. Moses, *Intel. Back.*, Chap. XI. Oyuela, I, 489–492. For further bibliography see Hills, *Odes,* 147–149.

** b. (VENEZUELA) **Andrés Bello** (1781–1865). Although born in Caracas, he may be considered a citizen of all South America because of his continental viewpoint and his long residence outside Venezuela. As a young lad, he laid the basis for his wide classical training by diligent study of Latin. He saved his pennies to buy the Spanish classics, read much, and gradually stocked his mind with encyclopedic knowledge. In 1810 he was sent to London as an agent of the revolting colonies to obtain funds. He remained there for nearly twenty years. These years he spent in study, literary investigation, and writing, supporting himself by tutoring. In 1826 he started a journal, *El repertorio americano,* through which he hoped to defend the cause of independence in the New World. In it he published for the first time his famous "Silva a la agricultura ..." In 1829, at the invitation of the new republican government, he went to Chile, occupying at first the post of Minister of Foreign Affairs. He spent the remainder of his very active life in Chile, being editor of *El araucano,* first president of the University of Chile, and a leader of the nation's intellectual life for many years. His amazingly varied labors included studies in law and philosophy, continued creative work in poetry, and the compilation of a

*Gramática castellana* which, with the notes of Rufino José Cuervo (Colombian, 1844–1911), is still considered the most complete and penetrating grammar of the language. During his life he was a defender of classicism and humanism, of authority in literature; as such he came into frequent conflict with Argentine exiles in Chile—among them the famous Sarmiento—who were fired with zeal for the literary theories of the romanticists. This polemic, violent and acrimonious at times, is one of the outstanding battles of American literary history. In his later years Bello composed, in imitation of Victor Hugo, one of his most lovely poems, "La oración por todos." His earlier "silva," while lacking the martial fervor of Olmedo's poem, shows a deeply patriotic concern for the future of the newborn republics and illustrates the idealistic and optimistic dreams which accompanied the independence movement.

SUGGESTED READING: (1) "Silva a la agricultura de la zona tórrida" (1826). (2) "La oración por todos" (1843).

TEXTS: Beltrán, *Antología,* I, 37–43 (2).[1] Hills, *Odes,* 27–41 (1). Hills and Morley, 214–220 (1, abridged). Holmes, *Span. Am.,* 503–506 (1, abridged). Menéndez y Pelayo, II, 301–312 (1). Monterde, 355–365 (1). Oyuela, I, 252–356 (1, 2, and others). Solar Correa, 26–31 (1, abridged). Valdaspe, 235–242 (1, abridged, and 2).

EDITIONS: *Obras completas,* Santiago de Chile, Consejo de Instrucción Pública, 1881–1893, Vol. III, *Poesías. Poesías,* precedidas de un estudio biográfico y crítico por M. A. Caro, Madrid, 1882 (Colección de escritores castellanos, III); reprinted, Barcelona, Maucci, 1909.

TRANSLATION: Walsh, *Hisp. Anth.,* 389–394 (1).

CRITICAL REFERENCES: Amunátegui, M. L., *Vida de Don*

---

[1] These numbers in parentheses refer to the corresponding selections in the Suggested Reading.

*Andrés Bello,* Santiago de Chile, 1882. ●Barrera, *Lit. hisp.,* 264–276. Beltrán, *Manual,* 75–81. Blanco-Fombona, 11–28. Giorgi, 81–88. Menéndez y Pelayo, II, cxvii–clviii. ●Oyuela, I, 492–502. For further bibliography see Hills, *Odes,* 141–146, and Waxman, Samuel, *A Bibliography of the Belles-Lettres of Venezuela,* Cambridge, Mass., Harvard University Press, 1935, 37–39.

** c. (CUBA) **José María Heredia** (1803–1839). Although not a poet of the Revolution (his country remained a Spanish colony until 1898), Heredia is considered here because he has characteristics in common with Bello and Olmedo and belongs to the same chronological period. He was born in Santiago, the son of a liberal father who taught him a hatred of political oppression. During his youth he lived in Venezuela (1812–1817) and Mexico (1818–1821). He returned to Cuba to finish his course in law and to practice there, but as a member of a revolutionary society he was involved in the first abortive movement to free Cuba from Spain and was sentenced to perpetual exile. He fled to the United States, where he spent two unhappy years, earning his living as a teacher of Spanish in a private academy in New York. After the publication of a volume of his poems in 1825, he went to Mexico, where he was appointed to several political offices. In 1836 he was allowed to return to Cuba, but he soon returned to Mexico and spent the three remaining years of his short life there.

Heredia is better known abroad than any other Spanish American poet of his period. His poems are classical in form but romantic in their intensity of emotion and their sense of intimacy between the experience of the poet and the moods of nature. Nearly all works of his youth, they are inspired by the grander forces of nature—the sea, the hurricane, the cataract—or by the poet's sense of time's pitiless antipathy to the works of man.

SUGGESTED READING: (1) "En el teocalli de Cholula" (1820). (2) "En una tempestad" (1822). (3) "Niágara" (1824). (4) "Al sol" (1825).

TEXTS: Beltrán, *Antología*, I, 52–57 (1 and others). Ford, 289–293 (2 and 3, abridged). Hills, *Bardos*, 2–33 (1, 2, 3, 4, and others). Hills, *Odes*, 85–116 (1, 2, 3, 4, and others). Holmes, *Span. Am.*, 262–265 (1, abridged). Menéndez y Pelayo, II, 15–46 (1, 2, 3, 4, and others). Oyuela, I, 357–374 (1, 2, 3, and others). Solar Correa, 32–37 (1). Torres-Ríoseco, *Antología*, 148–152 (1). Valdaspe, 246–247 (1 and 3, abridged).

EDITIONS: *Poesías*, New York, N. Ponce de León, 1875. *Poesías líricas*, Paris, Garnier, 1893. *Poesías, discursos y cartas*, 2 vols., Havana, Cultural, 1939.

TRANSLATIONS: Blackwell, 486–489 (4). Hills, *Odes*, 130–136 (3, trans. by William Cullen Bryant). Walsh, *Hisp. Anth.*, 405–414 (2 and 3). For other translations see González del Valle, Francisco, *Poesías de Heredia traducidas a otros idiomas*, Havana, 1940.

CRITICAL REFERENCES: Barrera, *Lit. hisp.*, 249–263. Beltrán, *Manual*, 94–96. Chacón y Calvo, José M., *Ensayos de literatura cubana*, Madrid, Calleja, 1922, 223–276. Menéndez y Pelayo, II, xiv–xxvii. •Oyuela, I, 502–507. •Zerolo, E., "Prólogo," Heredia's *Poesías líricas*, Paris, Garnier, 1893. For further bibliography see Hills, *Odes*, 150–153.

5. Representative authors of heroic poetry.

a. (ARGENTINA) **Esteban de Luca** (1786–1824). His entire life centered in the revolutionary movement in Argentina. Scarcely had he graduated from the Escuela de Matemáticas when his technical services were required for the establishment of factories for war materials. Most of the horseshoes for San Martín's trans-Andine campaign were turned out in the shops supervised by Luca. But he was skillful with words as well as with iron and wrote many odes and songs inspired by the martial deeds of San Martín and others. While still a young man, he lost his life in a shipwreck. His literary work was entirely patriotic in inspiration and is representative of that of dozens of other ardent young men of the period.

SUGGESTED READING: (1) "Canto lírico a la libertad de Lima" (1821). (2) "Al pueblo de Buenos Aires" (1822).

TEXTS: Barreda, I, 85–97 (1). Pagano, 239–244 (1, abridged). Puig, II, 191–220 (1 and 2).

CRITICAL REFERENCES: *García Velloso, 216–219. Giorgi, 107–110. Puig, II, xxxvii–lix. Rojas, "Los coloniales," 895–907.

b. (ARGENTINA) **Vicente López y Planes** (1784–1856) is known almost exclusively as the author of the Argentine national anthem, although his longer poem "Triunfo argentino," which tells of the repulse of the English invaders in 1810, has a documentary interest. During his whole life, he was active in national affairs as soldier, politician, and statesman.

SUGGESTED READING: "Himno nacional" (1813).

TEXTS: Barreda, I, 69–71. Laguardia, 1–6. Puig, II, 108–111.

CRITICAL REFERENCES: García Velloso, 154–162. *Rojas, "Los coloniales," 815–832.

c. (MEXICO) **Andrés Quintana Roo** (1787–1851). Typical of the impassioned spirit of the Mexican independence heroes was the life of this patriot. Writing heroic verse was only one of his many services to the cause. He was also a political journalist and statesman; his contribution to the independence of his country was recognized by the naming of a territory of the Republic in his honor. His verse is markedly classical in style, for, like most of the intellectuals of his time, he was steeped in Latin and Greek literature.

SUGGESTED READING: "Al 16 de septiembre de 1821" (1821).

TEXTS: Castro Leal, 63–68. Menéndez y Pelayo, I, 75–79. Oyuela, I, 375–380.

CRITICAL REFERENCE: Menéndez y Pelayo, I, xciii–xciv.

**6.** Popular verse of the Revolution.

Love songs in popular meters, a heritage of Spanish traditional folklore, were current among the common people during the colonial period. When the wars of independence enlisted the support of the masses, especially the gauchos in the La Plata region, the forms of popular poetry were used to express in simple, sometimes crude, language the hatred of the Spaniard and the glory of the Revolution. The commonest verse form was the "cielito." The directness and popular language of these songs are in marked contrast to the grandiloquence of the erudite heroic poetry.

REFERENCE: Rojas, "Los gauchescos," 433–461.

(URUGUAY) **Bartolomé Hidalgo** (1788–1822) was the most notable poet to imitate the popular gaucho verse for patriotic purposes. Born of humble parents in Montevideo, he was a bartender in his youth. Later he participated in the military operations of the independence movement. Aside from his *Diálogos,* his best-known composition, he wrote various "cielitos heroicos." He is often considered the first of the many gaucho poets of the early nineteenth century. (See Section C.)

SUGGESTED READING: "Diálogo patriótico" (1822).

TEXTS: Beltrán, *Antología,* II, 28–34. Henríquez Ureña and Borges, 47–56. Holmes, *Span. Am.,* 454–455 (abridged). Oyuela, I, 412–422.

CRITICAL REFERENCES: Oyuela, I, 515–531. Rojas, "Los gauchescos," 495–515 (life), 465–484 (works). •Zum Felde, *Proceso,* I, 69–80.

IV. Prose of the revolutionary period.

  1. Typical genres: oratory and journalistic essays.

  2. Representative writers.

   a. (ARGENTINA) **Bernardo de Monteagudo** (1785–1825) was born in Tucumán and educated in the colonial schools of Córdoba and Chuquisaca. He was among the first conspirators for independence in La Paz, where he was condemned to die as a traitor. Escaping, he joined the revolutionary army and later went to Buenos Aires. There he edited various revolutionary journals and wrote fiery, meaty articles on the problems of freedom. He continued his verbal campaigns in Chile and Peru, being for a time San Martín's secretary. He was one of the founders of the Sociedad Literaria Patriótica and did important work in a similar organization which he founded in Lima. While in Lima, he worked with Bolívar toward the formation of an American federation of states. Still at the height of a remarkable career, he died at the hand of an assassin in Lima.

   SUGGESTED READING: "Ensayo sobre la necesidad de una federación general entre los estados hispanoamericanos y plan de su organización" (1824).

   TEXTS AND EDITIONS: Rojas, Ricardo (ed.): Bernardo de Monteagudo, *Obras políticas,* Buenos Aires, Roldán, 1916 (Biblioteca argentina, VII), 75–88. *Escritos políticos,* prólogo del Dr. M. F. Rodríguez, Buenos Aires, Biblioteca "French," 1915, II, 243–266.

   CRITICAL REFERENCES: García Velloso, 172–181. Giorgi, 102–107. •Moses, *Intel. Back.,* Chaps. V, VII, IX. Rojas, "Los proscriptos," 62–80.

\*  b. (VENEZUELA) **Simón Bolívar** (1783–1830) as a writer. Great as were his military exploits, the Liberator is almost equally famous for his analyses of social and political conditions in the new republics. As García Calderón says: "He was the thinker of the Revolution... the first sociologist of these romantic democracies." His clear and energetic prose style is exemplified in his many letters and speeches, the best-known of which are the letter from Jamaica (a prophecy of future political conditions in Spanish America, 1815) and his draft of a model constitution offered to the Congress of Angostura.

SUGGESTED READING: "Discurso en el Congreso de Angostura" (1819).

TEXTS: *Address to the Venezuelan Congress at Angostura,* Cambridge, England, University Press, 1933 (Cambridge Plain Texts). Holmes, *Span. Am.* 547–548 (abridged).

EDITIONS: Blanco-Fombona, R. (ed.): Simón Bolívar, *Discursos y proclamas,* Paris, Garnier, 1933. *Cartas del Libertador corregidas conforme a los originales* ..., 10 vols., Caracas, 1929–1930. Simón Bolívar, *Selección* de Carlos Pellicer, México, Universidad Nacional, [1939].

TRANSLATION: Yanes, Francisco Javier (trans.), *An Address of Bolivar at the Congress of Angostura,* etc., Washington, D. C., B. S. Adams Press, 1919.

CRITICAL REFERENCES: •García Calderón, 69–80. Sánchez, *Hist. de la lit. am.,* 178–182.

** 3. (MEXICO) **José Joaquín Fernández de Lizardi** (1774–1827) is often known by his pseudonym, "El Pensador Mexicano." He was born into a middle-class family in Mexico City. Although his formal education was incomplete, he read widely in the French liberal authors and eagerly supported the revolutionary movement initiated by Hidalgo. Founding the revolutionary journal *El pensador mexicano* in 1812, he became famous as a violent propagandist and pamphleteer. His criticism of the authorities brought him to prison on several occasions. To the end of his life he was active in journalistic labors. Although he was essentially a journalist, his fame today rests largely on his picaresque novel, *El Periquillo Sarniento*, frequently called the first American novel. In it one finds "el mejor museo de nuestras costumbres en el ocaso virreinal" (González Peña). It has remained one of the most popular literary works in Mexico. Two other novels of his, *La Quijotita y su prima* (1819) and *Don Catrín de la Fachenda* (1825), show the same didactic criticism of morals as the *Periquillo*.

SUGGESTED READING: *El Periquillo Sarniento* (1816), Vol. III, Chap. I.

TEXTS AND EDITIONS: *El Periquillo Sarniento*, Barcelona, Sopena, 1908 (Biblioteca de grandes novelistas). For the many other editions see González Obregón, Luis, *Novelistas mexicanos: Don José Fernández de Lizardi*, Mexico City, Talleres Gráficos Linomex, 1938.

CRITICAL REFERENCES: González Obregón, *op. cit.*, 15–62 (biography). Spell, J. R., *The Life and Works of José Fernández de Lizardi*, Philadelphia, University of Pennsylvania Press, 1931, 9–54 (biography). Spell, J. R., "The Genesis of the First Mexican Novel," *Hispania*, XIV (1931), 53–58. Spell, J. R., "Mexican Society as Seen by Fernández de Lizardi," *Hispania*, VIII (1925), 145–165. Spell, J. R., "Fernández de Lizardi as a Pamphleteer," *Hispanic American Historical Review*, VII (1927), 104–123; on this topic see also Spell, *The Life and Works* etc., 92–110. For further bibliography see Spell, *The Life and Works* etc., 124–138.

# The Nineteenth Century before Modernism (1826–1888)

## BY E. HERMAN HESPELT

## INTRODUCTORY SUMMARY

At the close of the wars of independence the Spanish American countries found themselves faced with new political and cultural problems. For the next few decades—in some countries for the next half or three-quarters of a century—their principal political problem was the creation of stable and responsible national governments which could command respect abroad and ensure peace at home. Their principal cultural problem was the achievement of an intellectual life of their own, a literature and an art which should be rooted and grounded in the soil of the New World.

Great difficulties hampered and delayed the solution of both these problems. Before stable governments could be established, most of the newly formed "republics" were obliged to pass through a longer or shorter period of wars against their neighbor states and wars between factions within the state, followed inevitably by a period of military dictatorship. The economic and industrial development upon which alone the stability of a republican form of government can rest was retarded by a number of social factors, among which may be especially noted the racial heterogeneousness of the population, the absence of a large middle class of tradesmen and artisans, and the persistence of the aristocratic traditions that manual labor is degrading and that the natural resources of the land are rightfully the property of the rich and powerful. In spite of these handicaps some of the nations—notably Argentina and Chile—made

such progress through these years that they were able to enjoy a pro-
longed period of orderly, constitutional government.

The same influences which tended to prevent national political solidarity
tended also to prevent cultural independence. The very lack of a stable government was an influence in that direction. But other social habits and atti-
tudes helped to keep Spanish America intellectually a European colony
for an unduly long time. In most of the countries there was little or no
free public education. The percentage of illiteracy was very great; the
reading public was correspondingly small and was made up almost exclusively of the wealthy landholding families, government officials and
employees, army officers, priests, and an occasional merchant. These were
the people for whom books were written; they were also—with a few
notable exceptions like "Plácido" and Altamirano—the people by whom
books were written. Many of them were educated in Europe; all of them
felt themselves more closely related in taste and in breeding to the cultured classes of France and Spain than to the Indians and mestizos who
worked on their estates or in their mines; and all of them were accus-
tomed to import books and magazines from Europe along with the other
comforts and luxuries which gave novelty and interest to their lives. It
was very natural, therefore, that they should accept European styles in
thought as well as in dress and that each prevailing European literary
mode should be copied in its turn by Spanish American writers.

During the period under our consideration four such fashions in literature successively dominated the intellectual tastes of Europe and Spanish America: neoclassicism, romanticism, "costumbrismo," and realism.
The most important of these for the literary history of Spanish America in
the nineteenth century was romanticism. Neoclassicism was already in its
decline in the 1830's. It did little to encourage an original, American tone
in writing, and the works of many of its poets are indistinguishable from
those of continental Spaniards.

With the romanticists it is another story. Romanticism seemed made
to fit Spanish American temperaments and conditions. It stood for freedom, for individualism, and for emotional intensity. It exalted nature as
the source of poetic inspiration. It sought for its subject matter phases

of life remote in space or in time from the great centers of contemporary civilization. To the poets of Spanish America romanticism meant a new spirit of liberalism in literature and in politics, a spirit which was to find expression not only in their works, but in their lives. They felt themselves the custodians and defenders of liberty, called to work with other leaders of the state to create a new order. There were few of them who were not forced to suffer persecution or exile for their political beliefs; the most illustrious group, the famous Argentine proscripts, Echeverría, Mármol, and Ascasubi, continued to wage from their exile an unremitting and finally successful war against the tyrant Rosas.

In their works the romantic poets preferred to write on American themes. They composed long narrative poems called "leyendas" on heroic adventures from the past history of their countries, on native Indian legends, and on the great deeds of the recent wars. They wrote shorter lyrics on nature, on patriotism, and on love. Their favorite European models were Byron and Espronceda. Like them, they idealized and sentimentalized their heroes; like them, they allowed themselves freedom in metrical pattern, insisting that the verse form must be the direct reflection of the poet's feeling. Some of the romanticists wrote novels as well as poetry, taking as their models Chateaubriand and Hugo. In this genre, too, they wrote of the American scene, and these works, like their poems, show an intimate feeling for nature and a love of freedom.

Romanticism entered the various countries of Spanish America by different routes and at different times. It reached Mexico first in the early 1820's; by 1850 it had spread all over the southern continent. It continued to exert an influence on the American literary world until the closing decades of the century.

While romanticism was still young, another fashion in prose fiction, "costumbrismo," was imported into America by way of Spain. This was the fashion of writing short informal essays or sketches, "cuadros de costumbres," on various aspects of contemporary life: sketches without much plot or character interest which focused the reader's attention upon the setting—amusing or picturesque—of the small events they recorded. From the "cuadros" developed longer stories and novels of manners and customs which tried to reproduce the local color of a district or the provincial ways of a limited social group. Although the "costumbristas" were conscious imitators of a European school, their works, because of their choice of subject matter and their method of detailed description, are authentically American and present a more realistic picture of life in their native countries than can be found in the works of the romanticists.

The realism of the "costumbristas" was, however, a poetic realism. The starker realism of the naturalists appears in Spanish American literature only at the very end of our period, when the vogue of Zola was already well established in Europe.

Meanwhile there had developed in Spanish America two purely indigenous genres without prototype in the literatures of Europe. These were the "poesía gauchesca" of Argentine and Uruguay and the "tradiciones peruanas" of Ricardo Palma: the first, the literary flowering of a long oral tradition of folk tale and ballad; the second, the creation of a single man of genius.

The original "poesía gauchesca" was composed by the "payador" or gaucho minstrel and sung to the accompaniment of his own guitar as he wandered from place to place like the troubadours of the Middle Ages, but his songs were improvised, never recorded, and have been lost. The term "poesía gauchesca" is now given to poems written in imitation of his by educated men of letters who have succeeded in recapturing something of the spirit of his genuine "payadas." They celebrate the gaucho as lover, as poet, as outlaw. They are written in his own language. Their settings are the plains, the campfire, and the tavern. They owe their existence in part to the romanticists' interest in primitive nature and primitive man, but they are a very special outgrowth of the romantic spirit.

The "tradiciones peruanas"—as sophisticated as the "poesía gauchesca" is primitive—are in essence historical anecdotes based upon legendary or actual events in the history of Peru from the time of the Incas to the War of the Pacific (1879–1883), related with suavity and wit in a keen and limpid style. There is no doubt that they are related to the "cuadros de costumbres" in both form and subject matter, but Palma knew how to give his sketches a point or climax which the "cuadros" often lacked and how to draw a character or recreate a whole social era with a few deft lines. He may therefore fairly be said to have created a genre of his own.

These two new indigenous literary forms are the most significant contributions of Spanish America to world literature during the period of our study (1826–1888). They are indicative of the New World's growth in cultural independence during these years. But other works of the period are also a valuable part of the world's literary heritage. Isaacs' idyllic novel, the essays of Montalvo, and Sarmiento's *Facundo* have intrinsic as well as historical interest and continue to be read for their own sake. The works of some of the other writers—those of Mármol and Echeverría, for example—have already become old-fashioned and are interesting now chiefly for the light they throw on the ideas and tastes of their age or for their influence on later generations. A still larger number of poets, "costumbristas," and essayists, whose names have been omitted from our study, contributed much to the intellectual life of their own countries and still enjoy local fame, although they have failed to leave any permanent mark on the history of Spanish American letters.

General References: Barrera, *Lit. hisp.*, 293–441. Beltrán, *Manual*, Chaps. III–V. Coester, *Lit. Hist.*, Chaps. IV–XIV. Estrella Gutiérrez and Suárez Calimano, Chaps. III–V, VII–VIII, and X. Giorgi, 137–254. Sánchez, *Hist. de la lit. am.*, Chaps. X–XIV.

**I.** Historical background.

  **1.** Political, social, and economic obstacles to the establishment of stable national governments: lack of experience in self-government; idealistic, impractical constitutions; want of counterbalance to military power; racial mixture of population; inherited aristocratic traditions; high percentage of illiteracy; uneven distribution of wealth; absence of middle class; retarded industrial and commercial development.

2. The dictatorships.

   a. In Argentina and Uruguay.

   Juan Manuel Rosas becomes dictator of the La Plata provinces (1829).

   War breaks out between the federated provinces of Uruguay (1839).

   Siege of Montevideo (1842–1851).

   Rosas is defeated at Monte Caseros and goes into exile (1852).

   Struggle over "states' rights" between Buenos Aires and the provinces (1852–1862).

   b. In Peru.

   Ramón Castilla is president of Peru (1845–1851).

   Civil war (1854–1855).

   Castilla governs Peru as dictator (1855–1861).

   c. In Ecuador.

   Dictatorship of Gabriel García Moreno (1861–1875).

3. Juárez and Maximilian's Mexican empire.

   Annexation of Texas by the United States (1845).

   War between the United States and Mexico (1846–1848).

   General Santa Ana heads a conservative government in Mexico (1853).

   Benito Juárez, a Zapotec Indian, leads a revolt (1855).

   "War of Reform"; Juárez is head of the state (1857–1860).

   Great Britain, France, and the United States take over the Mexican customhouses (1860).

   French army invades Mexico (1862).

   French install Maximilian as emperor (1864).

   Juárez, supported by the United States, defeats Maximilian. Maximilian is taken prisoner and shot (1867).

4. Economic development and age of relative good order.

Election of Bartolomé Mitre as first president of an undivided Argentina (1862).

Election of Domingo Faustino Sarmiento to succeed Mitre (1868).

Death of Juárez in Mexico (1872).

Rule of Porfirio Díaz in Mexico (1876–1911).

War of the Pacific (1879–1883); Peru and Bolivia dispute Chilean claims to the nitrate provinces.

Chilean armies occupy Lima and burn the National Library (1881).

Treaty of peace between Peru and Chile (1883).

REFERENCES: Bryce, Chaps. XII–XV. •Chapman, *Rep. Hisp. Am.,* Chaps. I, VII–VIII. García Calderón, F., Book I, Chap. IV, Book II, Chap. V, Book III, Chap. I. Kirkpatrick, Chaps. XIII–XV, XXII, XXVIII. Rippy, Chaps. IX–XII. Shepherd, Chaps. VIII–XII. •Williams, Chaps. XV, XX, XXIII, XXV, XXIX.

II. Important factors influencing literature during the years 1826–1888.

   **1.** Limitations and character of the reading public.

   REFERENCES: Bryce, 519–520. Handman, Max, "Studies in Contemporary Mexican Literature," *Texas Review,* 1921, 169–175. Shepherd, Chap. XVI.

   **2.** European literary movements reflected or imitated in Spanish America.

   **a.** Neoclassicism.

   REFERENCES: Jiménez Rueda, *Historia,* 120–121. Peers, E. Allison, *A History of the Romantic Movement in Spain,* Cambridge, England, University Press, 1940, II, 59–68. Romera Navarro, *Historia,* 459–463.

   **b.** Romanticism.

   REFERENCES: Cejador y Frauca, VII, 2–14, 65–85. Jiménez Rueda, *Historia,* 144–149. Ospina, Eduardo, *El romanticismo,*

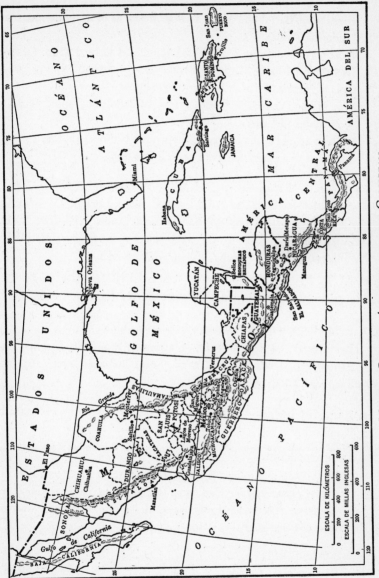

MEXICO, CENTRAL AMERICA, AND THE CARIBBEAN

*estudio de sus caracteres esenciales en la poesía lírica europea y colombiana,* Madrid, Voluntad, 1927. Rojas, "Los proscriptos," 419–428. Sánchez, *Hist. de la lit. am.,* 258–263, 303–306. •Tarr, F. Courtney, *Romanticism in Spain and Spanish Romanticism: A Critical Survey,* Liverpool, Institute of Hispanic Studies, 1939. Zum Felde, *Crítica,* 11–20.

**c.** "Costumbrismo."

REFERENCES: *Costumbristas y satíricos,* Paris, 1939 (Biblioteca de cultura peruana, 9), 15–17. •Spell, J. R., "The Costumbrista Movement in Mexico," *PMLA,* L (1935), 290–315.

**d.** Realism.

REFERENCES: Sánchez, *Hist. de la lit. am.,* 394–397.

**3.** The gaucho and his songs.

REFERENCES: Holmes, *Martín Fierro,* Chap. I. Hudson, W. H., *Far Away and Long Ago,* New York, The Modern Library, n.d., Chaps. V–XIII. Rojas, "Los gauchescos," Chaps. I, II. •Sarmiento, Domingo F., *Facundo,* Buenos Aires, La cultura argentina, 1925, Chaps. II, III. Zum Felde, *Crítica,* 109–127.

**III.** The poets.

**1.** The neoclassicists.

(ARGENTINA) **Juan Cruz Varela** (1794–1839) was born in Buenos Aires, but attended school in Córdoba, where he received a good classical training and was graduated with a degree in theology. His works fall into five periods: (1) works of his apprenticeship— translations from Vergil and Horace and early love poems; (2) two dignified tragedies in the classical tradition, *Dido* and *Argía;* (3) patriotic odes inspired by contemporary historical events; (4) poems on civic themes written in support of social reforms; and (5) his last and greatest poem, a song of exile, written a few months before his death after he had been banished to Montevideo. He was a man of true patriotism and sincere interest in culture; an intellectual, rather than an inspired poet.

SUGGESTED READING: (1) "Campaña del ejército republicano al Brasil y triunfo de Ituzaingó: canto lírico" (1827). (2) "El 25 de mayo de 1838, en Buenos Aires" (1838).

TEXTS: Barreda, I, 105–122 (1). Beltrán, *Antología,* I, 58–60 (2). Menéndez y Pelayo, IV, 91–95 (2). Oyuela, I, 428–441 (1 in part, and 2). Valdaspe, 42–47 (1 in part, and 2).

EDITIONS: *Poesías,* Buenos Aires, La cultura argentina, 1916. *Tragedias,* Buenos Aires, 1915 (Biblioteca argentina, 6).

TRANSLATION: Poor, 28–30 (2).

CRITICAL REFERENCES: Beltrán, *Manual,* 97–113. Estrella Gutiérrez and Suárez Calimano, 108–110. García Velloso, Chap. XVII. Menéndez y Pelayo, IV, cxxviii–cxliv. Oyuela, I, 534–545. Rojas, "Los coloniales," 945–985.

2. The romanticists.

** a. (ARGENTINA) Esteban Echeverría (1805–1851) was born in Buenos Aires. His father died while he was still young, leaving him to be brought up by an indulgent mother. From 1820 to 1823 he attended the Colegio de Ciencias Morales; in 1824 and 1825 he held a position with a commercial firm; then in 1826 he sailed for France. In France romanticism was at its height, and Echeverría became an enthusiastic disciple of the new faith which was to "break the chains of literary slavery." He read Shakespeare, Schiller, and Byron and began to write his first verses. He returned to Buenos Aires in 1830. In 1832 he published *Elvira o la novia de la Plata;* in 1834, *Los consuelos,* a collection of Byronic lyrics; and in 1837, *Rimas,* a volume containing his most famous poem, "La cautiva." The same year he founded the secret anti-Rosas society, "Asociación de mayo," before which he read his "Palabras simbólicas," a statement of the political principles of the young Argentine romanticists. He also worked at this time on "El matadero," a short story in prose, remarkable for its crude realism. After the revolution of 1839 he was obliged to flee to Uruguay, where he spent the last eleven years of his life, homesick and in ill health. During his exile he wrote several long poems—"La guitarra," "El ángel caído," and "Avellaneda" among them—but none equal in merit to his earlier works.

Echeverría was the first spokesman and program maker for the romanticists in Argentina. He was by nature an innovator and the leader of a school. He believed that America should break all spiritual ties with Spain and become wholly independent in its art. But he could not free himself entirely from his models; what he achieved was the substitution of French for Spanish masters.

Suggested Reading: "La cautiva" (1837).

Texts: Barreda, 195–253. Beltrán, *Antología*, I, 68–94. Holmes, *Span. Am.*, 11–13 (excerpt). Menéndez y Pelayo, IV, 175–238. Oyuela, II, vol. 1, 20–43 (excerpts). Valdaspe, 66–69 (excerpt). Weisinger, 56–73 (excerpts).

Edition: *La cautiva, seguido de El matadero, La guitarra, Elvira, Rimas,* Buenos Aires, Sopena, 1939.

Critical References: Beltrán, *Manual,* 119–134. Cejador y Frauca, VII, 152–158. Coester, *Lit. Hist.,* 107–113. Estrella Gutiérrez and Suárez Calimano, 118–128. García Velloso, Chap. XXI. Groussac, Paul, *Crítica literaria,* Buenos Aires, Jesús Menéndez e hijo, 1924, 279–320. Menéndez y Pelayo, IV, clxi–clxxx. Oyuela, II, vol. 2, 853–860. Rojas, "Los gauchescos," 689–714; "Los proscriptos," 240–317.

b. (Cuba) **Gabriel de la Concepción Valdés, "Plácido"** (1809–1844), was the illegitimate son of a mulatto barber and a Spanish dancer, brought up in a foundling home without any formal education. He earned his living by odd jobs and became a skillful carver of tortoise-shell combs. He read any books he could find, especially books of poetry, and was inspired by the works of Martínez de la Rosa to feel himself a poet. He chose "Plácido," the name of an apothecary who had befriended him, as his pseudonym. His poems were sporadically but not consistently successful, and in the periods between successes he wandered from town to town on the island without means and without recognition. In 1844 he was accused of complicity in a plot to bring about Negro domination in Cuba. He and ten companions were convicted and shot to death. On the way to his execution he recited the moving poems which he had composed during his imprisonment, insisting on his innocence and submitting himself to the will of God.

Plácido's fame rests upon the touching story of his life and upon a few poems of genuine feeling and inspiration. The bulk of his work is inferior in quality and taste. Although he does not treat specifically the problems of the colored race, his poems are protests against injustice and oppression.

SUGGESTED READING: (1) "Muerte de Gesler." (2) "A la fatalidad." (3) "Jicotencal." (4) "La flor de la caña." (5) "Plegaria a Dios" (1844).

TEXTS: De Vitis, 204 (5). Ford, 293–294 (5). Hills, *Bardos,* 34–43 (1, 2, 3, 5, and others). Hills and Morley, 190–191 (5). Holmes, *Span. Am.,* 266–267 (5). Menéndez y Pelayo, II, 69–84 (1, 2, 3, 4, 5, and others). Monterde, 183–184 (2). Oyuela, II, vol. 2, 490–498 (1, 3, 4, 5). Solar Correa, 53–54 (5).

EDITIONS: *Poesías completas con doscientas diez composiciones inéditas* ..., Habana, Alvarez Perez y Comp., 1886. *Poesías selectas de Plácido,* introducción por A. M. Eligio de la Puente, Habana, Cultural, S.A., 1930 (Colección de libros cubanos, 119).

TRANSLATIONS: Walsh, *Cath. Anth.,* 256–257 (5). Walsh, *Hisp. Anth.,* 431–433 (5).

CRITICAL REFERENCES: Coester, *Lit. Hist.,* 385–391. •García

Garófalo Mesa, M., *Plácido, poeta y mártir,* México, Botas, 1938.
•Menéndez y Pelayo, II, xxxiii–xxxviii. Oyuela, II, vol. 2, 952–954. Santos González, 253–294.

* **c.** (CUBA) **Gertrudis Gómez de Avellaneda** (1814–1873) lived in Cuba only until she was twenty-two years old. The rest of her life was spent in Spain—in Andalusia and Madrid—except for one visit to America in 1859. Most of her works were written and all were published in Spain, so they belong more properly to Spanish than to Spanish American literature except in so far as they are inspired or colored by the environment and experiences of her youth. She was not only a poet, but a dramatist and novelist as well. Her work in all three fields was very highly esteemed by her contemporaries, but it is chiefly for her poems that she is remembered today. Her best-known novels are *Sab* (1841), *Espatolino* (1844), and *Guatimozín* (1845); her greatest dramas, *Alfonso Munio* (1844), *Saúl* (1849), and *Baltasar* (1858). It has been said that the sources of her poetic inspiration are three: human love, divine love, and the love of her art. Her poems show real psychological insight and unusual skill in fitting form to mood.

SUGGESTED READING: (1) "A la poesia." (2) "A la muerte del célebre poeta cubano Don José María de Heredia." (3) "La pesca en el mar." (4) "La cruz" (1849).

TEXTS: Beltrán, *Antología,* I, 131–135 (1, 2). Hills, *Bardos,* 44–60 (1, 2, 3, 4). Holmes, *Span. Am.,* 269–271 (2). Menéndez y Pelayo, II, 87–121 (1, 2, 3, 4, and others). Oyuela, II, vol. 2, 499–531 (1, 3, 4, and others). Valdaspe, 248–249 (3, 4). Weisinger, 114–128 (1, 2, 4).

EDITION: *Obras de la Avellaneda,* edición nacional del centenario, 6 vols., Habana, A. Miranda, 1914.

TRANSLATIONS: Blackwell, 490–491. Poor, 50. Walsh, *Hisp. Anth.,* 434–436.

CRITICAL REFERENCES: Beltrán, *Manual,* 182–186. Cejador y Frauca, VII, 288–296. Chacán y Calvo, 187–219. •Cotarelo y Mori, Emilio, *La Avellaneda y sus obras,* Madrid, 1930. Menéndez y Pelayo, II, xl–xlvi. Oyuela, II, vol. 2, 954–958. Williams, Edwin B., *The Life and Dramatic Works of Gertrudis Gómez de Avellaneda,* Philadelphia, University of Pennsylvania, 1924.

**d.** (COLOMBIA) **José Eusebio Caro** (1817–1853) was born in Ocaña in Nueva Granada. Orphaned early, he had to earn his own living. He started to study law in Bogotá, but gave up his course to become a journalist instead. In 1836 he and his friend J. J. Ortiz founded a literary periodical, *La estrella nacional.* In 1837 he became sole editor of *El granadino,* a journal of political reform. He was elected deputy to the congress in 1841 and from then until 1849 held various posts of trust in public office. When a change took place in the government on the election of José Hilario López in 1849, he went as an exile to the United States for three years. As he was returning home in 1853, he contracted yellow fever, and died just as the ship reached the port of Santa Marta. He was a man of uncompromising moral integrity, a "Puritan" who repeatedly sacrificed personal advantage for principle, an ardent believer in political freedom and liberty of conscience. His greatest poems, some of which were written in exile, are all songs of freedom and the fearless man.

SUGGESTED READING: (1) "En boca del último Inca." (2) "La libertad y el socialismo." (3) "Despedida de la patria." (4) "El hacha del proscrito."

TEXTS: Beltrán, *Antología,* I, 136–138 (3). De Vitis, 201–202 (1). García Prada, 107–126 (1, 2 in part, 3, 4, and others). Holmes, *Span. Am.,* 215–217 (1, 3 in part). Menéndez y Pelayo, III, 25–54 (1, 2, 3, 4, and others). Monterde, 145–147 (4). Ortega, 118–122 (3 and others). Oyuela, II, vol. 1, 235–256 (1, 2, 4, and others).

EDITIONS: *Obras escogidas,* Bogotá, 1873. *Poesías,* Madrid, 1885 (Colección de escritores castellanos, 25).

TRANSLATIONS: Blackwell, 414–417 (1 with text). Walsh, *Hisp. Anth.,* 452–453 (1).

CRITICAL REFERENCES: Beltrán, *Manual,* 187–190. Coester, *Lit. Hist.,* 275–278. •Menéndez y Pelayo, III, xli–lii. Oyuela, II, vol. 2, 926–930.

  **e.** (ARGENTINA) **José Mármol.** See Section C, IV, 1, a.

3. Postromantic and eclectic poets.

*   **a.** (MEXICO) **Manuel Acuña** (1849–1873) was born at Saltillo. He entered the school of medicine at Mexico City in 1865. His scientific studies led him to a materialistic outlook on life, and an unhappy love affair completed his despair. At the age of twenty-four he committed suicide. Acuña was the author of one drama, *El pasado,* and one volume of poems, many of which are autobiographical.

    SUGGESTED READING: (1) "Ante un cadáver." (2) "Nocturno a Rosario."

    TEXTS: Hills and Morley, 202–206 (2). Holmes, *Span. Am.,* 358–360 (2). Menéndez y Pelayo, I, 263–270 (1, 2). Oyuela, III, vol. 1, 40–47 (1, 2). Solar Correa, 95–99 (1). Torres-Ríoseco, *Antología,* 179–183 (2). Weisinger, 158–167 (1, 2).

    EDITION: *Poesías,* con un prólogo de D. Fernando Soldevilla, octava edición aumentada con "El pasado," drama del mismo autor, Paris, Garnier, 1884.

    TRANSLATIONS: Blackwell, 154–156. Underwood, 291–298 (2 and another).

    CRITICAL REFERENCES: González Peña, 219–220. Jiménez Rueda, *Historia,* 194–195. Menéndez y Pelayo, I, cxlviii–cliii. Oyuela, III, vol. 2, 917–919. •Weisinger, 155–158.

**b.** (MEXICO) **Juan de Dios Peza** (1852–1910), Acuña's friend and schoolmate, was born in Mexico City. His father, who had been high in Maximilian's favor, lost his wealth and position after the fall of the empire. The son studied medicine at first, but gave it up to make his living in journalism. He became a prolific and popular poet. His works are uneven in quality. The best of them express with great tenderness and delicacy his love for his wife and his children. He collaborated with Vicente Riva Palacio in writing some versified *Tradiciones y leyendas mexicanas* (1884).

SUGGESTED READING: (1) "Fusiles y muñecas." (2) "En mi barrio." (3) "El visitador Múñoz" (1884).

TEXTS: Hills and Morley, 207–210 (1 in part, and others). Oyuela, III, vol. 1, 63–68 (1 and others), III, vol. 2, 927–929 (2). *Tradiciones y leyendas mexicanas* por Riva Palacio y Peza (ed. Romero de Terreros and Rosenberg), New York, Nelson, 1927 (3 and others). Weisinger, 168–179 (1 and others).

EDITION: *Poesías completas,* 5 vols., Paris, Garnier, 1891–1898.

TRANSLATION: Underwood, 311–315.

CRITICAL REFERENCES: Jiménez Rueda, *Historia,* 196. González Peña, 216–218. Oyuela, III, vol. 2, 925–930.

**c.** (ARGENTINA) **Olegario Victor Andrade** (1841–1882) was born in the province of Entre Ríos. Since his family was out of political favor, his formative years were spent away from the capital and in comparative poverty. At seventeen he left school without finishing his course and found employment in small government jobs and on newspapers in the provinces. This gave him a meager living, but left him no leisure for his real calling. Finally, at the comparatively mature age of thirty-six, he published his first great poem, "El nido de cóndores." This was followed during the next five years by four other major works: "Prometeo" (1877), "San Martín" (1878), "Victor Hugo" (1881), and "Atlántida" (1881). In 1880 Andrade was called to Buenos Aires and made editor-in-chief of *La tribuna nacional,* the government newspaper. He died two years later at the height of his fame and his creative power.

Andrade, like Walt Whitman, was filled with a vision of the great destiny awaiting his country. Like Whitman, he felt himself at once historian and prophet. Like Whitman, too, he used a broad canvas and heavy strokes to obtain his effects. His taste was not irreproachable, his diction sometimes vulgar, his figures awkward, his learning inadequate for his theme. But his message remains a source of noble inspiration for his countrymen.

SUGGESTED READING: (1) "El nido de cóndores." (2) "Prometeo." (3) "Atlántida: canto al porvenir de la raza latina en América."

TEXTS: Beltrán, *Antología,* I, 107–112 (1). Hills and Morley, 152–159 (2, 3 in part). Holmes, *Span. Am.,* 36–38 (1 in part). Menéndez y Pelayo, IV, 305–353 (1, 2, 3, and others). Monterde, 43–58 (3). Oyuela, III, vol. 2, 772–785, 1141–1159 (1, 2, and others). Solar Correa, 86–89 (3). Valdaspe, 133–135 (2 in part). Weisinger, 106–112 (1).

EDITION: *Obras poéticas,* Buenos Aires, La cultura argentina, 1915.

TRANSLATION: Walsh, *Hisp. Anth.,* 506–512 (3).

CRITICAL REFERENCES: Beltrán, *Manual,* 154–164. Estrella Gutiérrez and Suárez Calimano, 134–139. Menéndez y Pelayo, IV, clxxxvii–cxci. Oyuela, III, vol. 2, 1132–1140. Rojas, "Los modernos," 442–460. Valdaspe, 115–122. Valera, 97–152.

\* 

d. (URUGUAY) **Juan Zorrilla de San Martín** (1855–1931) was a native of Montevideo and received his early education there. He was sent to the University of Chile at Santiago to study law and completed his doctorate in 1877. The previous year he had published in Santiago his first book of verses, *Notas de un himno.* On his return to Uruguay he founded a daily paper, *El bien pú-*

*blico.* In 1879, at the unveiling of a monument to Uruguayan independence, he read in public the patriotic ode "La leyenda patria." The occasion is looked upon as a sort of poetic renaissance in Uruguay. Nine years later, after having suffered temporary exile and the loss of his beloved wife, he published his masterpiece, the epic *Tabaré.* From this time on he was showered with eulogies and honors. Equally gifted as orator and as poet, he filled with distinction many high public offices, serving successively as minister to Spain, to France, and to the Vatican. His later publications include *Resonancias del camino* (1895), a book of travel notes, *La epopeya de Artigas* (1900), a historical monograph, and *Conferencias y discursos* (1900), a collection of essays and addresses.

SUGGESTED READING:   (1) "La leyenda patria."   (2) "Tabaré."

TEXTS: Beltrán, *Antología,* I, 145–278 (2).  Beltrán, *Manual,* 196–197 (1 in part).   Holmes, *Span. Am.,* 456–457 (2, short excerpt).   Monterde, 313–320 (2, excerpts).   Oyuela, III, vol. 2, 603–636 (1, 2 in part).   Solar Correa, 100–105 (2, excerpts).

EDITION: *Tabaré: Novela en verso* and *La leyenda patria,* 3d ed., Barcelona, Ed. Cervantes, 1927 (Los príncipes de la literatura, VIII).

TRANSLATION: Blackwell, 444–446 (2 in part).

CRITICAL REFERENCES: Beltrán, *Manual,* 194–198.  García Calderón, *Semblanzas,* 151–159.   Oyuela, III, vol. 2, 1032–1037.   Valera, II, 263–290.   •Zum Felde, *Crítica,* 63–80.

4. Los poetas gauchescos.

a. (ARGENTINA) **Hilario Ascasubi** (1807–1875), born in Fraile Muerto (later Belle-Ville) in the province of Córdoba, led an exciting and adventurous life. When he was twelve years old, he ran away from school and joined the navy. His boat was captured and taken to Portugal, where he escaped, and, after traveling through France and England, he made his way home again.

He took part in the war against Brazil and was present at the battle of Ituzaingó. He was in prison for two years under Rosas, then escaped to Montevideo. Here he started a very successful bakery, using his profits to fit out a ship against the tyrant. During the siege of Montevideo he wrote and published in pamphlet form a series of "barrackroom ballads" purporting to be written by a gaucho in the army, dealing with life in the camp and on the battlefield, and fulminating against the dictator. These were collected under the title *Paulino Lucero, o los gauchos del Río de la Plata cantando y combatiendo contra los tiranos de las Repúblicas Argentina y Oriental del Uruguay* (1839–1851). After the defeat of Rosas (1852) he returned to Buenos Aires and started a periodical called *Aniceto el gallo,* which contained comments in prose and poetry on current political events and defended the political creed of the Unitarians. He also built a great theater, which burned down and ruined him financially. In 1860 he was sent by the government on a commission to Paris, and he remained there for many years finishing and publishing there his most important work, the gaucho epic, *Santos Vega o los Mellizos de la Flor* (1872), some fragments of which had appeared as early as 1851. The poem is now commonly known as *Santos Vega, el payador.*

SUGGESTED READING: *Santos Vega, el payador,* Cantos IX and X.

TEXTS: Beltrán, *Antología,* II, 45–258 (text of complete poem). Holmes, *Span. Am.,* 14–16 (excerpt from Canto IX). Oyuela, III, vol. 2, 666–670 (excerpt from Canto X). *Poetas gauchescos,* 103–245 (abridgment of complete poem).

EDITION: *Santos Vega, el payador,* texto completo, con una introducción de Carlos O. Bunge, Buenos Aires, La cultura argentina, 1915.

CRITICAL REFERENCES: Cejador y Frauca, VII, 135–137. Oyuela, III, vol. 2, 1076–1082. Rojas, "Los gauchescos," 621–645, 653–667,

669–688, 715–734. Tiscornia, E. F., "Introducción," *Poetas gauchescos*, 12–20, 31–34.

* **b.** (ARGENTINA) **Bartolomé Mitre** (1821–1906), one of Argentina's greatest statesmen, was poet and scholar as well. Born in Buenos Aires, he spent his childhood in the frontier town Carmen de Patagones, and his youth, except for a year on an Argentine ranch, in Uruguay. He enlisted at seventeen and won the rank of lieutenant colonel during the siege of Montevideo (1842–1851). In 1846 he published a volume of *Rimas* which contains most of his poetical works, including many execratory anti-Rosas verses and gaucho ballads. In 1847 his only novel, *Soledad,* appeared. The next few years he spent in Bolivia, Peru, and Chile. Of them he wrote: "I have made a long and wearisome pilgrimage, during which I have been journalist, novelist, soldier, educator, poet, engineer, and politician.... I have been the object of all sorts of honors, including those of persecution." He returned to take part in the final defeat of Rosas at Monte Caseros (1852). During the following years of dispute between Buenos Aires and the confederation of the other thirteen provinces he held in turn the positions of deputy, minister of war, and governor of Buenos Aires. In 1862 he became the first constitutional president of a united country. His term expired in 1868, and he was succeeded by Sarmiento. In 1874 he ran for re-election, was defeated, and disputed the election with an armed revolt. His men were beaten, and he was imprisoned for a time. His later years were devoted to historical and literary research, which bore fruit in a number of important works, such as the *Historia de Belgrano* (first published in 1858, but later revised), the *Historia de San Martín,* the *Carta sobre la literatura americana* (1871), and *Ollantay, estudio sobre el drama quecha* (1881).

SUGGESTED READING:   (1) "A Santos Vega."   (2) "El caballo del gaucho." (3) "El pato." (4) *Historia de Belgrano y de la independencia argentina,* "Introducción," Section IX.

Texts: Beltrán, *Antología,* III, 270–327 (4, complete introduction). Holmes, *Span. Am.* (3). Weisinger (1, 2, and others).

Edition: *Rimas,* 4th ed., Buenos Aires, La cultura argentina, 1916.

Translation: Blackwell, 382.

Critical References: Beltrán, *Manual,* 270–272. Cejador y Frauca, VII, 440–441. Estrella Gutiérrez and Suárez Calimano, 288–299. Kirkpatrick, 142–143. Rojas, "Los gauchescos," 918–928; "Los proscriptos," Chap. XX. •Rowe, L. S., *Bartolomé Mitre, 1821–1921: A Tribute to the Memory of the Great Argentine Statesman and Historian,* Washington, Government Printing Office, 1921.

** c. (Argentina) **Estanislao del Campo** (1834–1880) was born in Buenos Aires, the son of an army officer. He himself fought as captain on the side of the Unitarians in the civil wars against the confederation which followed the regime of Rosas. He later held various political positions, but his chief interest was literature. He was a disciple and follower of Ascasubi, choosing as his pseudonym "Anastasio el Pollo," reminiscent of "Aniceto el Gallo," but he surpassed Ascasubi in the sensitivity of his interpretation of the soul of the gaucho and in his innate good taste. He wrote many poems which do not belong to the "poesía gauchesca," but his masterpiece is "Fausto," a dialogue in which a gaucho describes his visit to a performance of Gounod's opera.

Suggested Reading: "Fausto" (1866).

Texts and Editions: Beltrán, *Antología,* II, 539–555. Oyuela, III, vol. 2, 1102–1110 (in part). *Poetas gauchescos,* 253–301. *Fausto, seguido de poesías completas,* Buenos Aires, Sopena, 1939 (Biblioteca mundial Sopena), 9–44.

Critical References: Beltrán, *Manual,* 213–218. Estrella Gutiérrez and Suárez Calimano, 197–201.  Oyuela, III, vol. 2, 1083–1102.  Page, F. M., "Fausto, a Gaucho Poem," *PMLA,* XI (1896), 1–62.  Rojas, "Los gauchescos," 735–756.  *Poetas gauchescos,* 21–26, 34–37.

** **d.** (ARGENTINA) **José Hernández** (1834–1886) was born on an estate in the province of Buenos Aires and grew up in the country among gauchos and Indians. He never attended school beyond the primary grades, but read voraciously and had a prodigious memory. During the civil wars he fought on the side of the Federals for the provinces. After their defeat he emigrated to Brazil for a time. Later he returned to Entre Ríos, Rosario, Montevideo, and finally Buenos Aires, where he founded the newspaper *Río de la Plata.* He subsequently held various positions in the government. In writing *Martín Fierro* (1872) and its sequel, *La vuelta de Martín Fierro* (1879), Hernández claims that it was his purpose to teach his unlettered countrymen to read by so imitating their manner of expression and their way of thought that reading would seem a natural continuation of their lives. He succeeded so well that the poems were to be found on sale in the humblest grocery stores in remote sections of the country. At the same time he accomplished with *Martín Fierro* the goal which Echeverría had set for himself in writing "La cautiva," the creation of a thoroughly American epic independent of European norms and influences.

Hernández also wrote a work in prose, *Instrucción al estanciero* (1881), which offered practical advice on problems of agriculture and animal husbandry.

SUGGESTED READING:   (1) *Martín Fierro.*   (2) *La vuelta de Martín Fierro.*

TEXTS AND EDITIONS: Beltrán, *Antología,* II, 295–535 (1, 2). Holmes, *Span. Am.,* 28–36 (1, short excerpt).  Oyuela, III, vol. 2, 713–771 (1, 2, in part).  Valdaspe, 146–148 (excerpts).  Weisinger, 94–104 (1, excerpts).  *Martín Fierro, La vuelta de Martín*

*Fierro,* Buenos Aires, La cultura argentina, 1919. *Martín Fierro,* comentado y anotado por Eleuterio F. Tiscornia, Tomo I, texto, notas y vocabulario, Buenos Aires, Imp. y casa ed. Coni Hnos., 1925. *Martín Fierro,* Buenos Aires, Lib. "La Facultad," 1937 (Biblioteca argentina, 19); introduction by Ricardo Rojas. *Martín Fierro,* Buenos Aires, Espasa-Calpe, 1938 (Colección austral, 8). *Martín Fierro y la vuelta de Martín Fierro,* Buenos Aires, Losada, [1939] (Grandes escritores de América, 1).

TRANSLATIONS: Owen, Walter (trans.), *The Gaucho, Martín Fierro,* New York, Farrar and Rinehart, 1936. Auslander, J. (trans.), *A Fragment from Martín Fierro* (*El gaucho*), New York, [Hispanic Society], 1932.

CRITICAL REFERENCES: Beltrán, *Manual,* 207–212. Estrella Gutiérrez and Suárez Calimano, 201–210. •Holmes, *Martín Fierro.* Oyuela, III, vol. 2, 1110–1132. Rojas, "Los gauchescos," 757–771, 772–814. Tiscornia, E. F., "La vida de Hernández y la elaboración de *Martín Fierro*" (introduction to *Martín Fierro y la vuelta de Martín Fierro,* Losada edition; see texts above), 7–22.

* **e.** (ARGENTINA) **Rafael Obligado** (1851–1920) was born in Buenos Aires and educated at the Colegio Nacional there. Possessing independent means, he was able to devote himself exclusively to literature. His collected poems were first published in 1885. He was one of the founders of the Faculty of Philosophy and Letters at the national university and was responsible for the establishment of the first chair in Argentine literature there. In a poetic contest with a contemporary poet, Calixto Oyuela, Obligado defended the romantic theory of poetry against the classical school. His poetic models were Echeverría, "Plácido," and Hernández. His poems may be divided into three groups: (1) poems in praise of the heroes of the wars of independence; (2) poems presenting intimate pictures of nature and human affection; and

(3) the *Leyendas argentinas,* poetic versions of Argentine folk legends, including four poems on the Santos Vega theme.

SUGGESTED READING: "Santos Vega: El alma del payador, La prenda del payador, El himno del payador, La muerte del payador" (1887).

TEXTS: Beltrán, *Antología,* II, 260–272. Holmes, *Span. Am.,* 38–40 (excerpt). Oyuela, III, vol. 2, 824–836 (in part).

EDITION: *Poesías,* edición definitiva dirigida por Carlos Obligado, Buenos Aires, Juan Roldán y Cía, 1923.

TRANSLATION: Blackwell, 348–377.

CRITICAL REFERENCES: Beltrán, *Manual,* 165–171. Cejador y Frauca, IX, 74, 79–80. Estrella Gutiérrez and Suárez Calimano, 139–143. Oyuela, III, vol. 2, 1164–1199. Rojas, "Los modernos," 478–499. Valera, 77–88.

## IV. The prose writers.

### 1. The romantic novelists.

**    a. (ARGENTINA) **José Mármol** (1817–1871) was born and educated in Buenos Aires. He early incurred the disfavor of the dictator, Rosas, was imprisoned in 1839, and, upon his release, fled to Montevideo, where a number of young liberal intellectuals had preceded him. In 1843, when Rosas's forces marched into Uruguay, Mármol escaped to Rio de Janeiro and shortly afterward set sail for Chile. His boat was caught in a terrible storm off Cape Horn and was forced to turn back to its home port. Mármol remained in Rio de Janeiro until 1846, returned then to Montevideo, and finally, after the overthrow of Rosas in 1852, to Buenos Aires. He was appointed to several public offices and in 1858 became director of the national library, a post which he held until his death.

Mármol has been called the "verdugo poético de Rosas" because of his bitter invectives against the tyrant. He is best known for his anti-Rosas poems and for *Amalia* (Part I, 1851; complete, 1855), the first novel of Argentina, which, despite its melodramatic plot and stilted dialogue, presents a powerful picture of life in Buenos Aires during Rosas's reign of terror. He was also the author of two romantic tragedies, *El poeta* (1842) and *El cruzado* (1851), of lyric poems of real merit, and of a longer poem in the style of Byron's *Childe Harold* called *El peregrino* (1847).

SUGGESTED READING: (1) *Amalia* (abridged edition). (2) "Rosas: El 25 de mayo de 1850."

TEXTS: Menéndez y Pelayo, IV, 265–304 (2 and others). Oyuela, II, vol. 1, 59–84 (2 and others). Solar Correa, 57–60 (2). Valdaspe, 73–82 (2 in part, and others). *Amalia* (ed. Leavitt), Boston, Heath, 1926 (1). *Amalia* (ed. Corley), New York, Macmillan, 1921 (1).

EDITIONS: *Amalia,* 2 vols., Leipzig, Brockhaus, 1877. *Poesías escogidas,* Buenos Aires, 1922.

TRANSLATIONS: Poor, 19–23 (2 and others). Serrano, Mary (trans.), *Amalia: A Romance of the Argentine,* New York, Dutton, 1919.

CRITICAL REFERENCES: Beltrán, *Manual,* 135–149. Cuthbertson, Stuart, *The Poetry of José Mármol,* Boulder, Colorado, 1935. Estrella Gutiérrez and Suárez Calimano, 128–132. Menéndez y Pelayo, IV, clxxxiii–clxxxvi. Oyuela, II, vol. 2, 868–908. Rojas, "Los proscriptos," Chap. XV. Torres-Ríoseco, *Novela,* 190–192.

b. (ECUADOR) **Juan León Mera** (1832–1894) was born in Ambato, a small town south of Quito. He received no formal schooling. From his early youth he was deeply interested in Indian lore. He published his first book of verse in 1858, a longer poem, *La virgen del sol,* in 1861, and *Cumandá,* his prose novel, in 1871. He was

also the author of a literary history of Ecuador and of other critical
and scientific studies. After he had gained fame as an author, he
received political appointments and honors. His novel, like those
of Chateaubriand and Cooper, his models, is extremely romantic in plot, his Indians highly idealized, but his feeling for the
grandeur of the primeval forest is sincere and his knowledge of
the folkways of the Indian, authentic.

SUGGESTED READING: *Cumandá o un drama entre salvajes,*
Chap. VII, "En el lago Chimano."

TEXTS AND EDITIONS: *Cumandá* (ed. Flores), Boston, Heath,
[1932]. *Cumandá o un drama entre salvajes,* Madrid, F. Fe,
1891.

CRITICAL REFERENCES: Barrera, *Lit. ecuat.,* 145–147. Barrera,
*Lit. hisp.,* 379–386. Coester, *Lit. Hist.,* 270–272. Meléndez, 151–
164. Valera, II, 211–221.

** c. (COLOMBIA) **Jorge Isaacs** (1837–1895) was the son of a prosper-
ous planter, an English Jew, who had come to Colombia from
Jamaica and married the daughter of a Spanish naval officer. He
was born in Cali and spent his childhood there and on his
father's estate on the slope of the Cordillera Central. In 1848 he
was sent to boarding school in Bogotá. He remained here for
six years. During this time his father's business ventures turned
unsuccessful, and the boy came home to find the family in
straitened circumstances. Soon afterwards both his parents
died. The civil war of El Cauca completed his financial ruin,
and he and his brothers and sisters were obliged to give up their
home and move to Bogotá. In this city he gained the approval
of the critics and the public by a volume of *Poesías* (1864). Three
years later (1867) he published his masterpiece, *María,* an idyllic
romance with many autobiographical features. *María* won immediate and continuing success and has been more widely read
than any other Spanish American novel. Isaacs was appointed
to several government posts, including that of consul to Chile.

He tried to win back his fortune by an ambitious business undertaking, but without success. His dream of owning again the home of his childhood never came true. He died in poverty.

The unique charm of *María* is due to a mingling of realistic detail and delicate, romantic melancholy.

SUGGESTED READING: *María* (abridged edition).

TEXTS AND EDITIONS: *María: Novela americana* (ed. Keniston), Boston, Ginn, [1918]. *María* (ed. Warshaw), Boston, Heath, [1926]. *María* (ed. Pitcher), New York, Macmillan, [1922]. *María*, Paris, Garnier, 1894. *María: Novela americana seguida de las poesías completas*, Buenos Aires, Sopena, [1938].

TRANSLATION: Ogden, Rollo (trans.), *María*, New York, Harper, 1890 (reprinted 1918).

CRITICAL REFERENCES: •Carvajal, Mario, *Vida y pasión de Jorge Isaacs*, Santiago de Chile, Ercilla, 1937. Popenoe, Wilson, "La casa de María," *Boletín de la Unión Panamericana* (Spanish edition), LV (1922), 56–64. Torres-Ríoseco, *Novela*, 194–197.

## 2. The "costumbrista" novelists.

*

a. (CHILE) **Alberto Blest Gana** (1830–1920) was born in Santiago, the son of an Irish professor of medicine. He began his career as a teacher of mathematics in the military academy. His first story was published in 1853. He was ambitious to record for posterity in imaginative prose the history of his country and the daily life of all classes of its people. In 1860 his *La aritmética en el amor* won the first prize ever offered in Chile for a work of prose fiction. It was followed by a series of other novels, the most important of which were *Martín Rivas* (1862) and *El ideal de un calavera* (1863). Thereafter Blest Gana entered the diplomatic service, serving many years as Chilean ambassador to France and to England. A second period of literary production began for him in 1897 with the historical novel *Durante la reconquista*. After his retirement from public life he lived in Paris and continued to write until an advanced age. His novels are social documents of the greatest interest and importance, but he lacked creative imagination. His influence upon his contemporaries was profound. He taught many of them to prefer prose to poetry.

SUGGESTED READING: *Martín Rivas* (abridged edition).

TEXTS AND EDITIONS: *Martín Rivas* (ed. Umphrey), Boston, Heath, [1926]. *Martín Rivas,* 2 vols., Paris and Mexico City, Bouret, 1924.

TRANSLATION: *Martín Rivas,* New York, Knopf, 1918.

CRITICAL REFERENCES: •"Alone" [H. Díaz Arrieta], *Don Alberto Blest Gana: biografía y crítica,* Santiago, Nascimento, 1940. Coester, *Lit. Hist.,* 224–228. Lillo, 131. Sánchez, *Hist. de la lit. am.,* 341–342. Torres-Ríoseco, *Novela,* 197–198. Umphrey, G. W., "Introduction," *Martín Rivas,* ix–xv (see texts above).

*

**b.** (MEXICO) **Ignacio Manuel Altamirano** (1834–1893) was a pure-blooded Aztec who lived until he was fourteen in a small Indian pueblo. Since he showed great precocity at the village school, he was sent to a larger town (Toluca) and finally to Mexico City to finish his education. Here his course of study was interrupted by the revolution of 1854, the "War of the Reform" (1857), and the war against Maximilian. Altamirano fought with the liberals under Juárez. After the expulsion of the French and the re-establishment of the republic he turned his interests to literature and education, edited the periodicals *Correo de México* and *Renacimiento,* founded literary societies, taught history and law, and by precept and example showed the younger generation of Mexican writers the value of the local customs, village types, and the stirring events of their own times as literary material. He was appointed consul-general in 1889 to Spain and later to France. He died in San Remo. His works include a volume of *Rimas* written before 1867 but published later (1871), the novel *Clemencia* (1869), the novelette *La navidad en las montañas* (1871), several short stories and "artículos de costumbres," and a posthumous novel, *El Zarco.*

SUGGESTED READING: (1) *La navidad en las montañas.* (2) *El Zarco.*

TEXTS AND EDITIONS: *La navidad en las montañas* (ed. Lombard and Hill), Boston, Heath, [1917]. *El Zarco: Episodios de la vida mexicana en 1861–63* (ed. Grismer and Ruelas), New York, Norton, [1935].

CRITICAL REFERENCES: González Peña, 211–214, 244–245. Iguíniz, 18–22. Jiménez Rueda, *Historia,* 186–189. Starr, 204–216. Torres-Ríoseco, *Novela,* 200.

3. The naturalists.

(ARGENTINA) **Eugenio Cambaceres** (1843–1888), a lawyer and politician, was the first novelist of importance to adopt naturalism in Spanish America. His earliest work, *Potpourri: silbidos de un vago* (1882), published anonymously, shocked literary circles in Buenos Aires by its frank discussion of subjects formerly considered unfit for print. His later books, *Música sentimental* (1884), *Sin rumbo* (1885), and *En la sangre* (1887), though they continued to treat of the more sordid aspects of life, were more kindly received, but still subjected to criticism.

SUGGESTED READING: *En la sangre,* Chap. XIII.

EDITION: *En la sangre,* Buenos Aires, Minerva, 1924.

CRITICAL REFERENCES: Holmes, *Span. Am.,* 58. Rojas, "Los modernos," 633–642. Torres-Ríoseco, *Novela,* 205–216.

4. History, essay, and "tradición."

a. (ARGENTINA) **Bartolomé Mitre.** See Section C, III, 4, b.

** b. (ARGENTINA) **Domingo Faustino Sarmiento** (1811–1888), the second great literary president of Argentina, Mitre's immediate successor in the office, was born in San Juan and grew up in the provinces. His schooling was irregular and intermittent, but he had a passion for learning and teaching and began to give instruction in the elementary school of San Luis at the age of fifteen. Since his political sympathies were "Unitarian," he left the country at the accession of Rosas (1829) and went to Chile, where he worked as rural schoolmaster, clerk, and miner. In 1837 he returned to his home province, where he organized a secondary school and founded a newspaper, *El zonda,* and was put in jail for the opinions expressed in it. He emigrated to Chile again in 1840 and again took up journalism and pedagogy, becoming director of the normal school in Santiago. From 1845 to 1848 he traveled extensively in Europe and the United States studying their educational systems. He returned to take part in the defeat of Rosas (1852). He subsequently served his province in the capacities of deputy, senator, minister, and governor, and was elected president of the Argentine Republic in 1868. After the conclusion of his term (1874) he devoted himself to the organization and improvement of the schools of the nation. He wrote prolifically on subjects connected with popular education —his collected works fill fifty-two volumes—but his place in the history of Spanish American literature depends upon his books of travel and reminiscence, *Viajes por Europa, Africa y América,* and *Recuerdos de provincia* (1850), and upon one volume of unique interest, *Facundo, o la civilización y la barbarie* (1845), his study of the career of one of Rosas's "caudillos" as seen against the background of Argentine history, customs, and temperament.

SUGGESTED READING:    *Facundo,* Chaps. I–III.

TEXTS AND EDITIONS: Laguardia, 22–73, 209–216 (excerpts). Holmes, *Span. Am.,* 56–58 (short excerpt). *Facundo,* con una introducción por Joaquín V. González, Buenos Aires, La cultura argentina, 1925. *Facundo,* Buenos Aires, Lozada, 1938 (Las cien obras maestras, 2).

TRANSLATIONS: Mann, Mrs. Horace (trans.), *Life in the Argentine Republic in the Days of the Tyrants, or Civilization and Barbarism,* New York, Hurd and Houghton, 1868. Frank, 127-151 (excerpt).

CRITICAL REFERENCES: Beltrán, *Manual,* 253-261. Cejador y Frauca, VII, 405-412. Coester, *Lit. Hist.,* 125-135. Estrella Gutiérrez and Suárez Calimano, 253-278. González, J. V., "Introducción," *Facundo* (see texts above). •Rojas, "Los proscriptos," Chaps. X-XII. Sánchez, *Hist. de la lit. am.,* 264-269.

\*  **c.** (ECUADOR) **Juan Montalvo** (1832-1889), born in the same year and in the same town as Juan León Mera, was an implacable enemy of tyrants and especially of his country's dictator, García Moreno. Possessing an extremely clear and flexible prose style, he used this gift to excoriate the ruler in the pages of his journal, *El cosmopolita.* Consequently he was forced to leave the country. When in exile in 1875, he heard that García Moreno had been assassinated, he is said to have exclaimed with satisfaction, "¡Mi pluma le ha matado!" After the tyrant's death he again found himself at odds with the authorities and was condemned to perpetual banishment. In 1880 his polemical essays were published in Panama under the title *Catilinarias.* From Panama he went to France, where he spent the rest of his life. Here he founded a paper called *El espectador,* and here his famous *Siete tratados,* written about 1873, were finally published in 1882. His remarkably successful imitation of *Don Quixote,* the *Capítulos que se le olvidaron a Cervantes,* appeared posthumously.

Montalvo's style has classic purity, balance, and perfection of form, but his spirit has no classical serenity; it is uncompromising and rebellious.

SUGGESTED READING: (1) "Washington y Bolívar." (2) "Elogio de la pobreza."

TEXTS: Beltrán, *Antología,* I, 117-118 (2). Holmes, *Span.*

*Am.* (1, in part).  Monterde, 227–235 ("De la risa").  Torres-Ríoseco, *Antología,* 125–128 (1).

EDITIONS:  *Capítulos que se le olvidaron a Cervantes,* Paris, Garnier, 1921.  *Geometría moral,* con una carta prólogo de Don Juan Valera, Madrid, Est. Tip. Suc. de Rivadeneyra, 1902.  *Siete tratados,* Paris, Garnier, 1921.

CRITICAL REFERENCES:  Barrera, *Lit. ecuat.,* 140–144.  Barrera, *Lit. hisp.,* 386–398.  Beltrán, *Historia,* 175–176.  García Calderón, *Semblanzas,* 201–206.  •Rodó, J. E., *Cinco ensayos,* Madrid, Ed. América, n.d. (Biblioteca Andrés Bello), 21–109.

d. (PUERTO RICO) **Eugenio María Hostos** (1839–1903) was the champion of union and independence for the Caribbean islands. He was born in Puerto Rico but educated in Spain and fought there for the republic of 1868. He hoped that republican Spain would give the Antilles the status of a free dominion within a vast federation of Spanish-speaking countries. Pérez Galdós mentions him in one of his *Episodios nacionales* (*Prim*) as a "young man of very radical ideas, talented and noisy." Banished from Spain, he came back to America, living first in the United States and then in many countries of Spanish America. In Santo Domingo he worked for the reform of the school system; in Chile he taught international law. Wherever he went he was a force for enlightenment and progress. His writings are concerned with problems of great social import; his style is that of an inspired teacher.

SUGGESTED READING:  *Moral social* (1888), "Prólogo de la primera edición" and Chap. XXVII.

TEXTS AND EDITIONS:  *Moral social,* Buenos Aires, Losada, 1939 (Grandes escritores de América, II), 15–17, 170–178.  Other selections from Hostos's works may be found in Beltrán, *Antología,* I, 124–130, and Holmes, *Span. Am.,* 314–316.

CRITICAL REFERENCES:  Beltrán, *Historia,* 179–181.  •Henríquez

Ureña, Pedro, "Ciudadano de América" (introduction to *Moral social;* see texts above). Sánchez, *Hist. de la lit. am.,* 375–377.

** **e.** (PERU) **Ricardo Palma** (1833–1919), Peru's greatest literary personality, was born in Lima and spent most of his long life in that city, absenting himself from it only for a short period of political exile in his youth and for brief interludes of travel in his riper years. He left the university before his graduation in order to give his attention to literature, journalism, and politics. He published his first book of verses, *Poesías,* in 1855. In 1863 his important historical study, *Anales de la Inquisición en Lima,* appeared; in 1865, another book of poems, *Armonías, libro de un desterrado;* and, in 1870, a third called *Pasionarias.* Two years later he found the medium which was to give him a unique place in Spanish American literature as the creator of the "tradición," or historical anecdote. In a series of nine volumes published intermittently from 1872 to 1910 Palma recreated with wit and imagination his country's past. During the wars with Chile (1879–1883) Palma's own house and manuscripts were destroyed and the books and documents of the Biblioteca Nacional plundered and scattered. On the conclusion of peace Palma was put in charge of the work of restoring the national library. He succeeded in recovering many of its treasures and in reviving and increasing its prestige. Thus, in a double sense, he may be said to have preserved the past for his fatherland. Palma started his literary career as a romanticist, but his temperament was not romantic, and his early poems have little value. He himself criticized them mercilessly. His muse was not lyrical, but ironic; not sentimental, but critical.

SUGGESTED READING: Selected "Tradiciones peruanas."

TEXTS AND EDITIONS: Beltrán, *Antología,* I, 119–122. Holmes, *Span. Am.,* 423–426. Torres-Ríoseco, *Antología,* 87–93. Weisinger, 129–154. *Las mejores tradiciones,* Barcelona, Maucci, n.d. *Tradiciones escogidas,* Paris, 1938 (Biblioteca de cultura peruana,

11). *Tradiciones peruanas,* Buenos Aires, Espasa-Calpe, 1939 (Colección austral, 132). *Tradiciones peruanas* (ed. Umphrey), Chicago, Sanborn, 1936. *Tradiciones peruanas,* edición publicada bajo los auspicios del Gobierno del Perú, 6 vols., Madrid, Calpe, 1924.

TRANSLATIONS: "The Knights of the Cloak," *Inter-America* (English edition), III (1920), 135–143. "Peruvian Traditions," *Inter-America* (English edition), V (1922), 251–256.

CRITICAL REFERENCES: Beltrán, *Manual,* 177–178. Cejador y Frauca, VII, 454–456. García Calderón, *Semblanzas,* 93–106. Leavitt, S. E., "Ricardo Palma," *Hisp. Amer. Hist. Rev.,* III (1920), 63–67. Palma, Angélica, *Ricardo Palma,* Buenos Aires, Tor, 1933. Torres-Ríoseco, *Novela,* 198–199. •Umphrey, G. W., "Introduction," *Tradiciones peruanas* (see texts above). Valera, II, 291–300.

# Modernism—Realism (1888-1910)

## BY JOHN A. CROW

## INTRODUCTORY SUMMARY

When modernism commenced its reaction against the stilted, outworn romantic and realistic traditions of the nineteenth century around 1880, the more important Spanish American countries had only recently passed from an epoch of chaotic revolutionary change into a fairly stabilized period of peace and prosperity. By 1888, the date of publication of Rubén Darío's *Azul,* which formally gave perspective to the "modernista" renovation, political stability was at least well enough established to permit the conception and rapid growth of a fundamental, widespread aesthetic movement. Foreign capital (British, North American, German), now somewhat safeguarded, was heavily invested in expanding the new economic frontier. France remained, as it had always been, the spiritual godmother of all the young Hispanic republics.

The United States, almost fully recovered from the reconstruction era following the Civil War, had become a wealthy, powerful economic unit under whose leadership in 1889 the first Pan-American Congress took place. For Spanish America, unfortunately, this became a symbol of North American hegemony over the western hemisphere, and at succeeding Pan-American gatherings unilateral restatements of the Monroe Doctrine further served to accentuate this feeling. By arrogating to itself (in fact if not in word) complete responsibility for Caribbean and sometimes for hemispheric law, order, finances, defense, and even government, instead of leaving that responsibility to a combination of American powers, the United

States often used the Monroe Doctrine as a pretext for intervention in its own behalf. This policy repeatedly inflamed Latin American public opinion, and was vigorously reflected in the works of many modernist writers: Darío, Rodó, Chocano, Ugarte, and others. Nevertheless, the influx of foreign capital helped increase upper-class wealth and leisure. The masses still lived in a state of peonage, but temporary economic stability quickly stimulated the growth of a "mentalidad tolerante y pseudoliberal, una literatura formalista y bizantina, y una política oligárquica," to use the words of the Peruvian essayist Luis Alberto Sánchez. Nationalism thrived in the political sphere, but not in modernist literature, which was held together and made international by the common Spanish heritage and the strong spiritual, educational, literary tutelage of France.

As the result of these things there was inaugurated a new cosmopolitan concept of culture and life in the community of Spanish American nations. In literature this expressed itself as a reaction against the previous period of realism. This negation was one of the elements which gave impetus, unity, and direction to stylistic refinements and the development of modernist aesthetic sensibilities; and, through modernist absorption of French influences plus a renewed interest in the Spanish classics, Spanish America was infused with a literary rebirth which in the end enabled it to discover its own authentic personality. The new movement was characterized by pessimism, refinements in language, the worship of beauty, the free use of new and revived old verse forms, and a notable amount of formalism. It was the first evidence of Ibero-American cultural maturity, and with it the Hispanic nations of the New World first entered the currents of universal literature. The generation of modernist aesthetes made fetishes of form, music, imagery, and stylistic innovations, but through strict practice of these literary exercises many of them acquired the technique for later playing a truly great music. In brief, modernism repeated for Spanish America of the late nineteenth century what Gongorism had done for Spain of the Golden Age. It is curious to note that the word itself "modernista," first used as a term of disparagement by critics of the movement, soon boomeranged and became a label of triumph. When modernism finally lost its appeal, it left behind an expanded horizon and a freshness, youth, exuberance, and vitality of both language and ideas which characterize the Spanish American literature of today.

Spain, France, and the United States were the principal foreign influences on Spanish American modernism, although nearly every European country left its mark on certain writers. The North American and French revolutions had been the inspiration for Latin American political freedom; French law, philosophy, and literature had inspired the great majority of Latin American writers since their struggle for independence, and many of these had lived and studied in Paris during their formative years. The impact of the United States was largely that of an economic colossus whose portrait was frequently (often unpleasantly) painted, and, except for an occasional moment inspired by Edgar Allan Poe or Walt Whitman, its literary influence was exceedingly small. On the other hand, the influence of several French writers was widespread and of great importance; they belonged mainly to three groups: the romantics (Hugo, Alfred de Musset, Lamartine, and others), who strongly affected the forerunners of the modernist movement; the Parnassians, seekers after the cold, technical perfection of art for art's sake, who were prominent in France during the 1860's (Gautier, Catulle Mendès, Baudelaire, Coppée, Sully-Prudhomme, José María de Heredia, Leconte de Lisle); and the symbolists, to whom shades, rhythm, music, and imagery were ideals, whose school commenced to hold sway around 1880 (Verlaine, Mallarmé, Maeterlinck). In Spanish American modernism these three influences were often so thoroughly fused that it was impossible to tell where one began and the other left off. It is also more or less arbitrary to divide the modernists into "precursors," "modernists proper," and "postmodernists," for many of them produced works which would belong under each of these three headings. Gutiérrez Nájera (Mexico), Julián del Casal (Cuba), and José Asunción Silva [1] (Colombia) are generally called the "precursors" of the movement, but they were full-fledged modernists in style. On the other hand, José Martí (Cuba), the fourth name ordinarily found among the "precursors," was not a modernist

[1] Nájera's life span was 1859–1895; that of Silva 1865–1896; Casal's 1863–1893; and Martí's 1853–1895.

in either ideology or style, although his influence in revitalizing and refurbishing the language and ideas of his generation was tremendous. In recapitulating the influences on modernism we must not forget that, though the shadow of France was omnipresent, the background of Spain was deeper, older, and of more enduring root. While the obvious markings were manifestly French, a host of Spanish authors—the primitives, the classic writers of the Golden Age, the romantic poets (Zorrilla and Espronceda), and above all the tenuous postromanticism of Gustavo Adolfo Bécquer—all flowed deeply in the main stream of modernist inspiration.

The three phases of modernism can best be traced if one takes the outstanding works of Rubén Darío, messiah of the movement, as examples of this development. *Azul* (1888), with its highly stylized tones of French exoticism, was mainly Parnassian and romantic. Juan Valera, the Spanish critic, noted and praised its cosmopolitan feeling and gave Darío a boost which added several palms to his poetic reputation. It was characteristic of modernism that Darío, a Nicaraguan, wrote and published French-permeated *Azul* in Chile, to have it analyzed and made famous by a critic of Spain, and finally to see it become a sort of genesis for the modernist revival throughout South and Central America and Mexico. No one reading *Azul* could find anything to identify it as the work of a Spanish American, certainly nothing to point in the direction of tiny nonliterary Nicaragua. Darío's second famous work, *Prosas profanas* (1896), represented modernism at its zenith, added the influences of symbolism to those of the Parnassians and romantics, and chanted a musical paean of nuances to the ivory tower, refuge of art. (It was Verlaine the symbolist who sang "music above all else, and after music, shade.") *Prosas profanas* was riding the high wave of popularity in Spanish America, Spain, and to some extent in France, when war broke out between Spain and the United States. The causes: overgrown Monroeism, the tyrannical Spanish regime in Cuba, the sinking of the battleship *Maine* in Havana harbor. The easily won victory for the United States, and the inglorious defeat of Spain, caused the Spanish American countries to feel a shudder of prophetic uneasiness at the newly crowned power of the colossus of the north, and made a "quiver of racial sympathy" for the mother country run through her former colonies. The war had no fundamental effect on modernist literature, but it did hasten somewhat the end of an unreal escapism, the sloughing off of altisonant excesses, and the getting down to earth of literary expression. The modernist writers, always thoroughly conversant with Spanish literature, now turned their attention more and more in that direction. Darío, for example, immersed himself in the poetry of the "cancioneros," the Spanish primitives, widened his reading of foreign poets, and came to the conclusion that simplicity and feeling were of greater worth than adornment. So in Darío's *Cantos de vida y esperanza* (1905) and *El canto errante* (1907) we see the end of modernist formalism, and the Galatean statue so delicately wrought in *Azul* and *Prosas profanas* (of which Darío had written, "se juzgó mármol, y era carne viva") now comes to life and breathes its new-found native soul into all twentieth-century Spanish American literature, with effects that reach back to Spain and France. Darío and the other modernists have at last fully realized the beauty, the literary possibilities, and the important problems of their native lands. No longer are they merely transient guests in a French cloister. Some critics have called this last phase of modernism "mundonovismo" (New-Worldism).

The publication of *Azul* in 1888 and its consequent popularity helped to launch a veritable swarm of short-lived Chilean, Argentine, and Mexican literary periodicals in the modern idiom. In Chile the literary weekly *Pluma i lápiz,* founded in Santiago in 1900, was the chief voice of these writers, none of whom gained a notable reputation until the end of modernism.

Other journals of this period, similarly inspired, were *La revista latina* and *La revista de América* (1896) of Buenos Aires, the latter founded by Rubén Darío and Ricardo Jaimes Freyre, and *La revista azul* (1894–1896) of Mexico, founded by Gutiérrez Nájera. More solidly established periodicals were *El cojo ilustrado* (1892–1915) of Caracas, which was more realistic ("criollista") than modernist, and *La revista moderna* (first epoch 1898–1903; second epoch 1903–1911) of Mexico, which was founded by Amado Nervo and Jesús E. Valenzuela. Another modernist journal of Mexico which deserves to be placed along with the *Revista azul* and *Revista moderna* in importance is the much overlooked *El mundo* (later *El mundo ilustrado*), which lasted from 1894 to 1914.[2]

Modernism was such a fertile epoch in Spanish American literature that it produced many excellent secondary writers who have necessarily been omitted from this section and will be listed here. Selections from the works of most of them may be found in the anthologies of the period. Leopoldo Díaz (Argentina) was an imitator of the French Heredia and Leconte de Lisle; Ismael Enrique Arciniegas (Colombia) was also a Parnassian (he translated the French Heredia's *Les Trophées* into Spanish); other writers were: (Mexico) Manuel José Othón, Francisco A. de Icaza, Luis G. Urbina, José Juan Tablada; (Argentina) Pedro B. Palacios ("Almafuerte"); (Santo Domingo) Fabio Fiallo; (Chile) Carlos Pezoa Velis, Luis Felipe Contardo; (Uruguay) Alvaro Armando Vasseur; (Peru) Ventura García Calderón (prose); and (Guatemala) Enrique Gómez Carrillo (prose).

Concomitant with modernism but with its source and the character of its expression at the opposite artistic pole, was realism, or "criollismo." The natural outgrowth of previous "costumbrismo," it was essentially American, regional, often naturalistic, always colloquial in style and content. In Argentina, Chile, and Mexico the movement was referred to as realism, regionalism, or naturalism, depending on its particular color. In Venezuela the term generally employed was "criollismo," and two Venezuelan semi-monthly literary journals were its principal exponents: the famous *Cojo ilustrado* (1892–1915) and *Cosmópolis* (1894–1898), both published in Caracas. Novels characteristic of the movement in Venezuela were *Peonía* (1890) by Vicente Romero García, which brought the word "criollismo" itself into general use, *El sargento Felipe* (1899), by Gonzalo Picón-Febres, and *Todo un pueblo,* or *Villabrava* (1899), by Miguel Eduardo Pardo.

In other South American countries many realist writers fell under the aegis of the nineteenth-century Spanish novelists Pérez Galdós, Valera,

---

[2] Other Mexican journals reflecting the growth of modernism were *El renacimiento* (second epoch 1894); *El tiempo* (literary supplement, 1891–1910); *México, revista de sociedad, artes y letras* (1892); *La revista nacional de letras y ciencias* (1889–1890); *El Fígaro mexicano* (1896–1897); and *El periódico de las señoras* (1896). In the provinces were the *Flor de lis* (1896–1897) of Guadalajara and *Bohemia sinaloense* of Culiacán.

Pereda, and Coloma. The two best-known authors of the group during the 1888–1910 period were Carlos María Ocantos of the Argentine and Lorenzo Marroquín of Colombia, the latter known for a single masterpiece, *Pax* (1907), which has been translated [3] into English under the same title.

In Mexico realism was unduly prolific and found a more than full expression in the milieu delineations, small-town tintypes, and windy sermonizings of Emilio Rabasa, López-Portillo y Rojas, and Rafael Delgado. The Spanish novelists Pereda and Galdós also exerted a general influence on these writers. Invaluable as a source for study of their times, these Mexican prose writers lacked the perspective which fine writing demands.

Another phase of realistic expression was the "literatura indianista," or literature of indigenous theme, which sprang full-bodied from the soil and soul of Peru, Bolivia, and Ecuador toward the close of the nineteenth century. Not until then did the myopic whites, the only group sufficiently educated to possess literary voice, manage to see beyond their proud city noses into the doglike lives of the exploited natives. This indigenous element comprised (and still comprises) from sixty to eighty per cent of the population of the three so-called "Indian countries" of South America. These natives lived far better under the Inca rule than in 1900 after nearly four centuries of Spanish civilization and Christianization. The "literatura indianista" represented a complete about-face from the romanticism of Mera's *Cumandá* (1871). This new "Indianist" feeling sifted from the top downward until eventually it permeated the social, economic, moral, and political structure of these three countries. Mexico, after the regime of Porfirio Díaz, was to get a strong taste of the same thing. Clorinda Matto de Turner of Peru (1854–1909), first great feminine champion of Indian rights, started the swing in a native direction with her novel, *Aves sin nido* (1889), about the exploitation of the Peruvian natives. Manuel González Prada, also of Peru, treated among the modernist essayists of this section, carried a similar torch, which he hurled with devastating effect into many a neatly piled heap of Latin American prejudices.

In the "rioplatense" region (Argentina, Uruguay) realism often took on

[3] By Isaac Goldberg, Brentano's, New York, 1920.

a regional, gaucho background. The famous gaucho epic, *Martín Fierro* (1872–1879), had summarized and given literary perspective to an epoch which was already past, and in the succeeding generation, when this epic broke up into its component elements, it marked the course to be followed by the drama, short story, poetry, and novel of that region for some time to come. As in the case of other great epics—the *Poem of the Cid, Beowulf,* the *Song of Roland*—this expansion and projection of the seed in *Martín Fierro* was the most important stage in the unfolding of a great national literature in Argentina and Uruguay.

In the theater realism produced no significant works of merit except in the River Plate region. This so-called "teatro rioplatense" had its origin in the gaucho pantomimes and crude melodramas which were a feature of the circus rings of Argentina and Uruguay toward the close of the nineteenth century (beginning about 1884). Legendary gaucho heroes (Juan Moreira, Santos Vega, Martín Fierro) were generally the protagonists. At first these dramatic representations were very rudimentary and had no set scripts, but gradually they expanded and took on form and color, some of them were written down, and a new type of drama was born. The second, or "city," era of the new drama began in 1902 with the presentation of *Jesús Nazareno* by Enrique García Velloso. These "city dramas" (not always on city themes) were of known authorship, frequently treated the gaucho, and often dealt with rural and urban social or moral problems.

In summary, during the period when the ivory tower encaged modernist art, realism was hard put to shake off its own European shibboleths, and made only a perfunctory contribution to Spanish American *belles lettres.* These first insecure steps of its nineteenth-century childhood, however, were soon to become the brisk, bold strides of the strong maturity characteristic of Latin American literature today.

General References:   Aita, A., "El significado del modernismo," *Nosotros,* LXXI (1931), 361–371. Argüello, Santiago, *Modernismo y modernistas,* 2 vols., Guatemala, 1935. Blanco-Fombona, R., *Letras y letrados de Hispano-América,* Paris, Ollendorff, 1908. •Blanco-Fombona, *El modernismo.* Blanco García, M., *Los voceros del modernismo,* Barcelona, 1908.

Cejador y Frauca, Vol. X.   Coester, *Lit. Hist.*, Chap. XIV.   Estrella Gutiérrez and Suárez Calimano, Chap. VI.   García Calderón, V., *Del romanticismo.*   García Calderón, V., *Semblanzas.*   García Godoy, F., *La lit.
amer.*   García Godoy, F., *Americanismo literario.*   •Goldberg, *Studies.*
Gómez Carillo, E., *El modernismo,* Madrid, 1905, reprinted 1914.   "Lauxar"
[Osvaldo Crispo Acosta], *Motivos.*   •Meza Fuentes, *De Díaz Mirón a
Rubén Darío.*   •Onís, *Antología.*   Pérez Petit, V., *Los modernistas,* Mon-
tevideo, 1903.   Rohde, Jorge Max, *Las ideas estéticas en la literatura argen-
tina,* Buenos Aires, 1921, I, 259–312.   Sánchez, *Hist. de la lit. am.,* Chaps.
XV–XVII.   Santos González,   *Poetas.*   •Torres-Ríoseco,   *Precursores.*
Torres-Ríoseco, *Novelistas contemp.*   Umphrey, G. W., "Fifty Years of
Modernism in Spanish American Poetry," *Modern Language Quarterly,*
I (1940), 101–114.   Valera, *Cartas americanas,* I.   Zum Felde, *Crítica,*
199–204.

**I.** The historical background (1888–1910).

    **1.** Dictators and conservatism.
     Porfirio Díaz in Mexico (ruled 1876–1911).
     Rafael Núñez (poet-president) in Colombia (1880–1894).
     Guzmán-Blanco of Venezuela followed by Cipriano Castro (1899–
       1908) and Juan Vicente Gómez (1908–1935), last of the "old line"
       tyrants.
     Nicolás Piérola in Peru (1895–1899).
     José Manuel Balmaceda in Chile (1886–1891).
     Conservative presidents in Argentina; growth of political power
       of "radicals."
     Many writers of the period subsidized by these dictators, some
       given well-paid diplomatic positions: Rubén Darío, Ricardo
       Jaimes Freyre, Amado Nervo, Enrique González Martínez, Leo-
       poldo Lugones, and others.

    **2.** Birth and sad youth of Pan-Americanism.
     First Pan-American gathering in Washington, D. C. (1889).

SOUTH AMERICA TODAY

Spanish-American War in 1898; Spain's last New World colonies (Cuba and Puerto Rico) freed from European domination.

United States intervention in Latin America, sometimes invoking Monroe Doctrine, always letting it hang over Latin American heads like the sword of Damocles; in Venezuela (1896) against Great Britain; in Venezuela (1903) against Germany; in Panama (1903) against Colombia; other interventions in Antilles and Central America; growing storm of protest in Latin America (Manuel Ugarte, Rubén Darío, Rufino Blanco-Fombona, José Santos Chocano, José Enrique Rodó).

United States capital invested in Latin America grows rapidly: sugar in Cuba; copper and nitrate in Chile; silver, copper, and oil in Peru; bananas in Central America; silver, oil, industries in Mexico. Many high-interest loans made to Latin American governments; in order to ensure collection United States bankers often got firm hold on Latin American customs, taxes, finances.

3. Awakening of Latin American social consciousness.

Gradual evolution of Latin American nations from military dictatorships to civil governments.

Slow, oftentimes hardly perceptible growth in national concern for the huge masses of landless workers despoiled by old Spanish colonial system of latifundia and more recent era of "caudillos" or military dictators backed by large land-owners.

CRITICAL REFERENCES: Chapman, *Rep. Hisp. Am.*, Chaps. VII–X. •García Calderón, F., Book V, Chap. II. Rippy, Chaps. X–XII. Shepherd, Chaps. XX–XXI. •Williams, Chaps. XVII–XXXIII.

II. Important factors influencing literature.

1. Foreign influences tending toward modernism.

REFERENCES: •Contreras, Francisco, *Pour l'élargissement de l'influence française dans l'Amérique du Sud,* Paris, 1919. Darío,

Rubén, *Historia de mis libros,* Buenos Aires, 1912. Díez-Canedo, E., "Relaciones entre la poesía francesa y la española desde el romanticismo," *Revista de libros,* Madrid, 1914, No. 8, 55-65. García Calderón, V., *Del romanticismo.* •Henríquez Ureña, Max, "Las influencias francesas en la poesía hispanoamericana," *Revista iberoamericana,* II (1940), 401-419. •Mapes, *L'influence française.* •Monterde, Francisco, "Consideraciones sobre el modernismo," *Memoria del Primer Congreso Internacional de Literatura Iberoamericana,* Mexico, 1939, 123-129. •Monterde, Francisco, "La poesía y la prosa en la renovación modernista," *Revista iberoamericana,* I (1939), 145-151. Salinas, Pedro, "El cisne y el buho," *Revista iberoamericana,* II (1940), 55-79. Symons, Arthur, *The Symbolist Movement in Literature,* New York, 1919; excellent general study of French symbolists. Torres-Ríoseco, *Precursores.* Valera, I. Warshaw, Jacob, "Góngora as a Precursor of the Symbolists," *Hispania,* XV (1932), 1-14. •Zérega-Fombona, A., "El simbolismo francés y la moderna poesía española," *Cultura venezolana,* XIV (1922), 260-277; XV (1923), 66-77.

2. Foreign influences tending toward realism.

REFERENCES: •González Peña, 211-265. •Ratcliff, Chaps. V-IX. Rojas, "Los modernos." Silva, L. Ignacio, *La novela en Chile,* Santiago, 1910. Starr, *Readings.* Torres-Ríoseco, *Novela,* 199-224. •Torres-Ríoseco, *Novelistas contemp.,* 213-271. Urbina, Luis G., *La vida literaria de México,* Madrid, 1917.

3. Native influences.

REFERENCES: •Guzmán, 25-119. •Cometta Manzoni. •Meléndez, 171-178. Rojas, "Los proscriptos" and "Los modernos." Sánchez, *Hist. de la lit. am.,* 394-444. Torres-Ríoseco, *Novela,* 210-240. Torres-Ríoseco, *Novelistas contemp.,* 11-151.

4. The theater.

REFERENCES: Beltrán, Oscar, *Los orígenes del teatro argentino,*

Buenos Aires, 1934, 99–156. •Bianchi, Alfredo A., *Teatro nacional,* Buenos Aires, 1920. •Bierstadt, Edward H., *Three Plays of the Argentine,* New York, 1920; contains a study and three plays translated into English. Bosch, Mariano G., *Historia del teatro en Buenos Aires,* Buenos Aires, 1910. Echagüe, Juan Pablo, *Teatro argentino (impresiones de teatro),* Madrid, 1917. Giusti, Roberto F., "El drama rural argentino," *Nosotros,* V [2nd series] (1937), 241–264.

## III. Modernism.

### 1. The precursors.

General characteristics: transition from romanticism to modernism marked by infiltration of French influences; style, free flowing, musical; approach, subjective, pervaded with melancholy; use of new verse forms.

** a. (MEXICO) **Manuel Gutiérrez Nájera** (1859–1895) attended a French school as a child, wrote verses at an early age, and later became a journalist, editor, poet, and prose modernist. He established Mexico's first "modernista" journal, the *Revista azul,* in 1894, and continued it until his death. Nájera was hideously ugly in body, and given to heavy drink. Many of his finest poems show that he was constantly beset by an unresolved religious conflict. His work is deeply permeated with French influences (Alfred de Musset, Gautier, Verlaine). Nájera's whimsical, highly colored sketches and stories exerted great influence on modernist prose. He often used the pen name "El Duque Job," which is suggestive of his temperament (the aristocrat—the sufferer). The importance of his work lies in that it best represents the transition between romanticism and modernism. Both his prose and his poetry are restrained, elegiac, spontaneously musical, pervaded with delicate elegance and melancholy.

SUGGESTED READING: "Serenata de Schubert," "Para entonces,"

"De blanco," "Pax animae," "Non omnis moriar," and other poems. Among his stories "Rip-Rip."

TEXTS: Coester, *Anthology*, 6–26. Holmes, *Span. Am.*, 364–367. Onís, 5–21. Oyuela, II, vol. I, 69–105. Torres-Ríoseco, *Antología*, 169–171. Torres-Ríoseco and Sims, 41–49. Weisinger, 180–198.

EDITIONS: There was no edition of poems in the author's lifetime. *Poesías*, Mexico, 1896; prologue by Justo Sierra. *Obras completas*, 4 vols., Mexico, 1898–1910. *Sus mejores poesías*, Madrid, [1916] (Biblioteca Andrés Bello, LXXIV); appreciation by Rufino Blanco-Fombona. *Cuentos de color de humo y Cuentos frágiles*, Madrid, 1917. *Sus mejores poesías*, Mexico, 1933.

TRANSLATIONS: Blackwell, 2–33. Underwood, 5–33. Walsh, *Hisp. Anth.*, 551–558. Walsh, *Cath. Anth.*, 326–327.

CRITICAL REFERENCES: Blanco-Fombona, R., "Ligera apreciación sobre Gutiérrez Nájera," *Sus mejores poesías* (see editions above), 9–41. •Blanco-Fombona, *El modernismo*, 69–87. Goldberg, 16–46. González Peña, 228–230. •Meza Fuentes, 37–55. •Onís, 5–7 and 1175; extensive bibliography. Oyuela, III, 930–947. Santos González, 399–422; the essay is by Justo Sierra. Torres-Ríoseco, *Precursores*, 49–74. Walker, Nell, *The Life and Works of Manuel Gutiérrez Nájera*, Columbia, Missouri, 1927.

b. (MEXICO) **Salvador Díaz Mirón** (1853–1928), who was once a member of the Mexican Congress, led a stormy and dramatic life. An impulsive sense of honor caused him to fight duels and suffer imprisonment. He lived entirely apart from literary currents of his day in aristocratic seclusion—a man of extremely broad and profound culture. Díaz Mirón began his literary life as an admirer of Byron and Victor Hugo, and progressed toward a desire for perfect expression (often enigmatic and abtruse) which at times recalls Góngora. He did not belong clearly to any modernist group. His work exerted a considerable influence on Rubén Darío and José Santos Chocano, particularly the poem "A Gloria," which was known and often quoted by all modernists. The later poems of Díaz Mirón, which were collected in a volume entitled *Lascas* ["Chips from a Stone"] (1901), show perfected form at its zenith.

SUGGESTED READING: "A Gloria," "El fantasma," and other poems.

TEXTS: Coester, *Anthology*, 3–6. Holmes, *Span. Am.*, 360–362. Onís, 54–64. Oyuela, III, vol. 1, 139–146.

EDITIONS: *Poesías*, Mexico, 1886; Nueva York, 1895. *Lascas*, Xalapa, 1901. *Poemas escogidos*, selección de R. López, Mexico, 1919. *Sus mejores poemas*, prólogo de R. Blanco-Fombona, Madrid, n.d.

TRANSLATIONS: Underwood, 35–38. Walsh, *Hisp. Anth.*, 535–537.

CRITICAL REFERENCES: •Blanco-Fombona, *El modernismo*, 51–69. González Peña, 230–231. •Meza Fuentes, 13–37. •Monterde, Francisco, "Algunos puntos oscuros en la vida de S.D.M.," *Memoria del Segundo Congreso Internacional de Catedráticos de Literatura Iberoamericana*, Mexico, 1941. Onís, 54–55 and 1178; extensive bibliography.

** c. (CUBA) **José Martí** (1853–1895), patriot, journalist, essayist, critic, poet, symbol of Cuban struggle for independence, exile, revolutionary worker, national martyr, and hero. He resided and wrote successively in Mexico (1874–1877), Guatemala, Spain, New York, Venezuela (1877–1880), and again in New York (1881–1895), where he remained to work for the cause of Cuba until his final departure to take part and die in the last war for his country's freedom. Martí's poetry is of a sincere simplicity unparalleled save in folk ballads; it does not enter at all into the torrent of modernist formalism. He is considered a precursor of the modernist movement because of his disregard for the flamboyant and stilted characteristics of nineteenth-century literature. His articles (written mainly for *La nación* of Buenos Aires between 1882 and 1891) bear on every conceivable subject and are couched in a style that is deeply original and personal; his letters form a category unique in the Spanish language. His works as a whole mix influences of Spanish classic and popular culture and of England and North America, and show no decided characteristics of any literary movement. His literary work, great as it is, is hardly the equal of his life, which is the shining ideal of all Cubans.

SUGGESTED READING: "Versos sencillos," Nos. 1, 7, 9, 23, 39. Prose selections "Nuestra América" and "Los Pinos Nuevos" in the collection of M. Henríquez Ureña.

TEXTS: Holmes, *Span. Am.*, 279–283. Onís, 34–49; poetry only. Torres-Ríoseco, *Antología*, 167–168.

EDITIONS: *Versos sencillos*, New York, 1891. *Versos*, Buenos Aires, 1919; notes by Rubén Darío. *Poesías*, Havana, 1929; edited by Juan Marinello. *Páginas escogidas*, Paris, 1923; edited by M. Henríquez Ureña. *Páginas selectas*, Buenos Aires, 1939; edited by Raimundo Lida. *Nuestra América*, Buenos Aires, Losada, 1939. *Obras completas*, Madrid, 1925; edited by A. Ghiraldo. *Obras completas*, Ed. Trópico, Havana, 1936; edited by Gonzalo de Quesada y Miranda; some 30 volumes published to date.

TRANSLATIONS: Charles, C. (trans.), poems, in C. Charles, *Fuya....*, New York, 1898.

CRITICAL REFERENCES: •Beltrán, *Manual*, 220–225. Goldberg, 46–52. Hernández Catá, A., *Mitología de Martí*, estudio histórico, Madrid, 1929. Lizaso, Félix, *Martí, místico del deber*, Buenos Aires, Losada, 1940. •Meza Fuentes, 55–69. •Onís, 34–37 and 1176–1178; extensive bibliography. •Torres-Ríoseco, *Precursores*, 77–93.

* **d.** (Cuba) **Julián del Casal** (1863-1893) was born and died in Havana, Cuba. His health was undermined by a painful form of tuberculosis which made of him an almost morbid introspectionist. He had a thorough acquaintance with the French Parnassian movement, and poems reflecting this contact appeared in the journal *La Habana elegante* and other periodicals beginning in 1885. Casal was a great lover of exoticism and Japanese art, a deep admirer of Baudelaire, an excellent Parnassian sonneteer. His poems are a most intense expression of desolation, irony, emptiness. Both metrically and in feeling these writings are strongly characteristic of the coming "modernista" renovation.

SUGGESTED READING: "Páginas de vida," "Nostalgias," "Recuerdo de la infancia," "Rondeles" (I, II, and III), and other poems.

TEXTS: Coester, *Anthology,* 27-37. Holmes, *Span. Am.,* 284-285. Onís, 64-78. Oyuela, III, vol. 1, 267-270.

EDITIONS: *Hojas al viento,* Havana, 1890. *Bustos y rimas,* Havana, 1893. *Sus mejores poemas,* Madrid, 1916; a critical edition by Rufino Blanco-Fombona.

TRANSLATIONS: Walsh, *Cath. Anth.,* 337-338. Walsh, *Hisp. Anth.,* 564-569.

CRITICAL REFERENCES: •Blanco-Fombona, *El modernismo,* 87-103. Cejador y Frauca, X, 115-116. Goldberg, 52-57. •Meza Fuentes, 95-111. Nunn, Marshall, "Vida y obras de Julián del Casal," *América,* Havana, IV (1939), October. •Nunn, Marshall, "Julián del Casal, First Modernista Poet," *Hispania,* XXIII (1940), 73-80. Onís, 64-66 and 1178; extensive bibliography. Oyuela, III, vol. 2, 986-989. Torres-Ríoseco, *Precursores,* 35-47.

** **e.** (Colombia) **José Asunción Silva** (1865-1896), born of good family into an environment of culture, was both as child and as man deeply fascinated by the fairy tales of Grimm and Andersen. He visited France in 1886, and returned to narrow provincial Bogotá as one who was prison-bent. During the next ten years he produced many of the finest, most spiritually nostalgic, most pessimistic of modernist poems. His suicide at the age of thirty-two cut short a poetic career of tremendous promise; his talents might easily have made him Spanish America's greatest poet.

Silva's father died leaving many business debts which the son assumed and unsuccessfully struggled to pay off; he received a further rebuff from fate when the ship carrying his manuscript to France was lost at sea. After his sister's death the poet sank into morose melancholy, remembered her in beautiful, plaintive Nocturno III, one of the most famous "modernista" poems. Nearly all of his poetry is marked by pessimism, recollections of childhood, an ironic tinge, and the intense lyric expression of a frustrated soul attempting to retain childish illusions in maturity only to see them "fade into the light of common day." Silva committed suicide by firing a bullet into his heart. He was a perfectionist whose world of books could not long endure the battering of a hostile and narrow realism. His fluid use of old and new verse forms did much to liberate Spanish American poetry. Postromantic kinship with Heine, Poe, Baudelaire, Bécquer, and Campoamor make Silva the most typical of the creators of the new modernist lyricism, as he was also the most consummate voice in forming its melancholy language.

SUGGESTED READING: "Crepúsculo," "Nocturnos" I and III, "Día de difuntos," "Los maderos de San Juan," "Psicopatía," and other poems.

TEXTS: Coester, *Anthology,* 38–56. Holmes, *Span. Am.,* 228–229. Onís, 79–94. Oyuela, III, vol. 1, 568–576. Torres-Ríoseco, *Antología,* 172–174.

EDITIONS: There was no edition of Silva's poems during his lifetime. *Poesías,* Barcelona, 1908; contains excellent critical study on poet by Miguel de Unamuno. *Poesías,* edición definitiva, Santiago de Chile, 1923; prologue by Baldomero Sanín Cano. *De sobremesa,* Bogotá, 1925; prose.

Translations: Blackwell, 402–413. Craig, 32–37. Walsh, *Cath. Anth.,* 339–340. Walsh, *Hisp. Anth.,* 581–588.

Critical References: •Blanco-Fombona, *El modernismo,* 103–147. Goldberg, 57–64. •Meza Fuentes, 69–95. Onís, 79–80 and 1178–1179; extensive bibliography. Oyuela, III, vol. 2, 1024–1026. Sanín Cano (see editions above). Torres-Ríoseco, *Precursores,* 95–124. Unamuno (see editions above).

2. The modernist poets.

General characteristics: chiseled style, philosophy of the ivory tower, triumph of perfected form, innovations of new rhythms and revival of old, fusion of Parnassian art form with symbolist cult of music. The modernists develop more fully all the tenets of their precursors, from whom they differ only in degree.

**     a. (Nicaragua) **Rubén Darío** (1867–1916) was born in the village of Metapa, Nicaragua, of Spanish-Indian-Negro extraction. He became Spanish America's most followed, most cosmopolitan poet. The child's parents were separated, and Rubén was reared by an aunt. He wrote verses in early childhood, became known as "el poeta niño," imitated Bécquer and Campoamor, and acquired a wide Spanish and French culture. His literary talents were soon recognized and to some extent subsidized by influential Central Americans. He traveled over Central America and in 1886 went to Chile, where he worked on *La época* of Santiago, immersed himself in contemporary French literature (Flaubert, Catulle Mendès), and won a poetic contest. In 1888 there appeared in Chile his *Azul,* a famous collection of verse and prose sketches which set the stage for modernism in Spanish America. Juan Valera, writing in Madrid's *El imparcial,* pointed out the young poet's "galicismo mental," cosmopolitan spirit, Parnassian style. *Azul* was pure "art for art's sake" painted against a background of pagan mythology permeated with a sensuous awareness of color and sound, but often expressed in terms of a French formalism suggesting the gardens of Versailles. Darío next commenced to write for *La nación* of Buenos Aires, with which great paper he remained connected until his death twenty-six years later. In 1890 he returned to Central America and married unhappily; in 1892 *La nación* sent him to Spain, where he met many famous Spanish men of letters. He returned to America via Cuba, and in Colombia met Rafael Núñez (poet and former president of that nation), who secured his appointment as Colombian consul in Buenos Aires. Darío then headed for Argentina via New York (where he met Martí) and Paris (where he met intoxicated Verlaine and other French writers). His next famous work, *Prosas profanas* (1896), marks the zenith of the "modernista" movement; the imprisoned princess in the poem "Sonatina" becomes symbolic of the fettered modernist aesthetic creed encaged in cold marble. In 1898 Darío returned to Spain for *La nación* and wrote a series of articles on European subjects. In 1905 appeared his finest work, *Cantos de vida y esperanza,* which retains all the beauty of his former periods plus a great new feeling of freedom, simplicity, strength. The poet then returned to South America (Rio de Janeiro and Buenos Aires), and in 1908 was appointed Nicaraguan minister to Spain. As a result of heavy drinking his health began to fail. In 1915 he visited the United States on a lecture tour and failed miserably. Soon afterward he caught pneumonia in New York and rallied only sufficiently to return to Nicaragua, where he died in 1916.

Darío's influence on modernism was tremendous. He was the chief inaugurator, most famous exponent, guiding genius and messiah of the movement; through him Hispanic poetry was born anew. He was "el poeta de América" because of that supremely American characteristic of fusing all sources, inspirations, feelings, bloods, into one spiritual sensibility which was and is the secret of America's great cosmopolitan crucible. The letter of American content has been more fully developed by other poets, particularly Chocano, but Darío gave it life.

SUGGESTED READING: "La reina Mab" and other prose sketches. "Caupolicán," "Walt Whitman," "Sonatina," "Yo soy aquel ...," "A Roosevelt," "Los cisnes," "Canción de otoño en primavera," "Lo fatal," and other poems.

TEXTS: Beltrán, *Antología*, I, 362–450, contains all of *Azul*, as well as selections from other works. Coester, *Anthology*, 57–136. *Selections from Prose and Poetry of Rubén Darío* (ed. Umphrey and García-Prada), New York, Macmillan, 1928. *Poetic and Prose Selections of Rubén Darío* (ed. Rosenberg and López de Lowther), Boston, Heath, 1931. Holmes, *Span. Am.*, 119–128. Onís, 143–197. Oyuela, III, vol. 1, 198–242. Torres-Ríoseco, *Antología*, 175–180.

EDITIONS: *Primeras notas*, Managua, Nicaragua, 1885. *Azul*, Valparaíso, 1888. *Azul ...*, Buenos Aires, Espasa-Calpe, 1939 (Colección austral, 19). *Prosas profanas*, Buenos Aires, 1896. *Cantos de vida y esperanza*, Madrid, 1905. *Cantos de vida y esperanza*, Buenos Aires, Espasa-Calpe, 1940 (Colección austral, 118). *El canto errante*, Madrid, 1907. *Historia de mis libros*, Buenos Aires, 1912. *Obras escogidas*, 3 vols., Madrid, 1910; with a study by A. González Blanco. *Obras completas*, 22 vols., Madrid, Mundo Latino, 1922. *Obras completas*, 15 vols., edited by Alberto Ghiraldo and Andrés González Blanco, Madrid, Renacimiento and Biblioteca Rubén Darío. *Obras completas*, 31 vols., published by his son Rubén Darío Sánchez, Madrid, 1922. *Obras poéticas completas*, prologue by Alberto Ghiraldo, Madrid, 1932.

TRANSLATIONS: Blackwell, 182–201. Craig, 38–75. Walsh, *Cath. Anth.*, 347–351. Walsh, *Hisp. Anth.*, 595–613. Walsh, Thomas, and de la Selva, Salomón, *Eleven Poems of Rubén Darío*, New York and London, Putnam, 1916.

CRITICAL REFERENCES: •Blanco-Fombona, *El modernismo*, 147–191. Cejador y Frauca, X, 73–115. •Contreras, Francisco, *Rubén Darío: su vida y su obra*, Barcelona, 1930; pp. 315–319 contain bibliography of editions and criticism. Darío,' *Historia de mis libros*, Buenos Aires, 1912. García Godoy, 3–44. Goldberg, 101–183. Lugones, Leopoldo, *Rubén Darío*, Buenos Aires, 1919. •Mapes, *L'influence française*. Meza Fuentes, 111–354. •Onís, 143–156 and 1180–1181; extensive bibliography. Oyuela, III, vol. 2, 969–984. Rodó, J. Enrique, *Hombres de América*, Montevideo, Claudio García, 1939, 246–294 (date of first publication 1920). Santos González, 423–476; essay by Rodó. •Torres-Ríoseco, *Rubén Darío, casticismo y americanismo*, Cambridge, Mass., 1931; pp. 243–253 contain an excellent bibliography. Valera, I, 267–294.

**b.** (COLOMBIA) **Guillermo Valencia** (1872– ) is of an aristocratic family, and received a strict classical education. He once ran for the presidency of his country. He is simple and democratic in temperament and on one occasion remarked that he would rather be a good general or doctor than a writer. Valencia in some ways is the most Parnassian of all writers in Spanish, but his style suggests a mixture of Greek and Latin classicism plus its later Spanish heritage more than French Parnassianism. His ideology is not based on cold objectivity but is rooted in sensitive human values and feelings; he was never a professional writer.

SUGGESTED READING: "Leyendo a Silva" and "Los camellos."

TEXTS: Coester, *Anthology*, 167–178. Holmes, *Span. Am.*, 235–236. Onís, 347–365. Torres-Ríoseco, *Antología*, 186–187.

EDITIONS: *Ritos*, Bogotá, 1898. *Ritos*, 2d ed., London, 1914; considerably enlarged, and with an introduction by Baldomero Sanín Cano; this edition also contains several translations from Hugo, Verlaine, Wilde, D'Annunzio, Eugenio de Castro, and others.

*Catay*, 1928; "tradiciones chinas," but style makes it an original work. *Sus mejores poemas*, Madrid, 1919.

TRANSLATIONS: Blackwell, 412–415. Craig, 112–125. *Translations from Hispanic Poets*, New York, [Hispanic Society], 1938, 209–211. Walsh, *Cath. Anth.*, 386.

CRITICAL REFERENCES: •Blanco-Fombona, *El modernismo*, 221–237. Coester, *Anthology*, 300–304. Onís, 347–348 and 1184; extensive bibliography. Ortiz Vargas, A., "Guillermo Valencia, Colombia's Master Poet," *Poet Lore*, vol. 41 (1930), 413–423. Reid, John T., "Una visita a D. Guillermo Valencia," *Revista iberoamericana*, II (1940), 199–201. Sanín Cano, Baldomero, "Guillermo Valencia," *Revista de América*, February, 1913 (also see editions above).

c. (BOLIVIA) **Ricardo Jaimes Freyre** (1872–1933), teacher, diplomat, and one-time Bolivian Minister to the United States, was for several years a professor of history and literature at the University of Tucumán. He lived for an extended period in Buenos Aires, where he and Darío founded the *Revista de América* in 1896. His first work, *Castalia bárbara*, 1899, was his best; it marks a step in the development of modernism, and its aptly chosen title is characteristic of the poet's fusion of "Castalia" or classic "fountain of the gods" with elements of barbaric splendor. Freyre lived and wrote apart from reality in a fantastic, mythological world which was more Germanic than Hellenic, more of the Nordic Middle Ages than of the Italian Renaissance.

SUGGESTED READING: "Aeternum Vale," "Siempre (Paloma imaginaria)," "Hoc Signum," "El canto del mal (II)."

TEXTS: Coester, *Anthology*, 137–141. García Calderón, V., *Cuentos*, 160–167. Holmes, *Span. Am.*, 102–103. Onís, 365–369.

EDITIONS: *Castalia bárbara*, 1899. *Los sueños son vida*, 1917. *Los más bellos poemas de R. Jaimes Freyre*, prologue by Leopoldo Lugones, Mexico, Cultura, 1920.

TRANSLATIONS: Blackwell, 454–461. Craig, 85–88.

CRITICAL REFERENCES: Blanco-Fombona, *El modernismo,* 341–345. Lugones, Leopoldo; see editions above. Onís, 365 and 1185; extensive bibliography. •Torres-Ríoseco, "Ricardo Jaimes Freyre," *Hispania,* XVI (1933), 389–398.

** d. (ARGENTINA) **Leopoldo Lugones** (1874–1938), most famous Argentine modernist, was a close friend of Darío. For several years he directed the National Council of Education in Argentina, and was once the representative of his country on the Committee on Intellectual Co-operation of the League of Nations. He made various trips to Europe. Lugones expressed a dislike for Spain, a fondness for France and the United States, and he extolled Pan-Americanism. His ideology evolves from socialism to nationalism, and from romanticism to realism. The many facets of his literary expression presage and give base to the later phases of modernism; he can be simple, complex, romantic, symbolistic, or rigorously real as the mood strikes him. He is perhaps the most varicolored of all modernists except Darío, and some critics place him along with that famous Nicaraguan above all the others, call him the exponent of a new "culteranismo literario."

SUGGESTED READING: "Las montañas de oro" (fragmentos), "Delectación morosa," "A los gauchos," "La blanca soledad," "Elegía crepuscular," and other poems.

TEXTS: Coester, *Anthology,* 142–147. Holmes, *Span. Am.,* 44–46. Noé, 13–85. Onís, 369–396. Torres-Ríoseco, *Antología,* 191.

EDITIONS: *Las montañas de oro,* Montevideo, 1897; appreciation by Rubén Darío. *Los crepúsculos del jardín,* Buenos Aires, 1905. *La guerra gaucha,* 1905; prose. *Odas seculares,* 1910. *Historia de Sarmiento,* Buenos Aires, 1911; prose. *Rubén Darío,* Buenos Aires, 1919; prose. *Las horas doradas,* Buenos Aires, 1922. *Cuentos fatales,* Buenos Aires, 1924; prose. *Romancero,* Buenos Aires, 1924. *Poemas solariegos,* Buenos Aires, 1928.

TRANSLATIONS: Blackwell, 326–338. Craig, 96–111. Brenner, A. (trans.), "Death of a Gaucho," in Frank, 81–102 (story from *La guerra gaucha*). Walsh, *Hisp. Anth.*, 664–670.

CRITICAL REFERENCES: *Babel*, Buenos Aires, No. 19, May, 1926; dedicated to Leopoldo Lugones. •Blanco-Fombona, *El modernismo*, 295–341. Cossío, C., "La nueva generación y Leopoldo Lugones," *Nosotros*, L (1925), 98–105. Echagüe, Juan Pablo, *Seis figuras del Plata*, Buenos Aires, 1938, Chap. II. •Estrella Gutiérrez and Suárez Calimano, 359–367. "Lauxar," 177–198. Mas y Pi, Juan, *Leopoldo Lugones y su obra*, Buenos Aires, 1911. *Nosotros*, número extraordinario dedicado a Lugones, VII [second series] (1938). •Onís, 369–372 and 1185; extensive bibliography. Uriarte, G., "The Intellectual Work of Leopoldo Lugones," *Inter-América* (English edition), II (1919), No. 6.

**      **e.** (MEXICO) **Amado Nervo** (1870–1919) studied for the priesthood but left the seminary to become a journalist in Mazatlán. He visited Paris in 1900, where he met Darío. Nervo wrote for the *Revista azul* as long as it lasted, and when this journal died, Nervo and Jesús E. Valenzuela established the *Revista moderna* (1898–1903), the second famous modernist periodical of Mexico. Besides poetry Nervo wrote short stories, literary criticism, essays, prose poems in considerable number, a long study on Sor Juana Inés de la Cruz. From 1905 to 1918 the poet was secretary to the Mexican legation in Madrid, where much of his best work was produced; in 1919 he went to Argentina and Uruguay as Mexican Minister and died in Montevideo in 1919. His writings are characterized by a growing pantheism, Buddhistic feeling, touches of mystic serenity, a deep religious sentiment despite outward skepticism, and an almost Indian resignation and humility. His poetry shows a slow progression from overadornment and frivolity to simplicity, depth, perfection. The titles of his best works are fully characteristic of their content.

SUGGESTED READING: "La hermana agua," "A Kempis," "Expectación," "Si eres bueno," "Inmortalidad," and other poems. "Una esperanza" (a short story).

TEXTS: Beltrán, *Antología*, I, 450–470; contains all of *Serenidad*, and also other poems. Coester, *Anthology*, 211–230. Crow, *Cuentos hispánicos*, 25–33. Holmes, *Span. Am.*, 371–375. Onís, 396–416. Oyuela, III, vol. 1, 150–198. Torres-Ríoseco and Sims, 19–27. Wilkins, 62–72.

EDITIONS: *Poemas*, Paris, 1901. *Serenidad*, Madrid, 1914. *Elevación*, Madrid, 1916. *Plenitud*, Madrid, 1918. *La amada inmóvil*, Madrid, 1920. *La amada inmóvil*, Buenos Aires, Espasa-Calpe, 1939 (Colección austral, 32). *Los cien mejores poemas de Amado Nervo*, prologue by Enrique González Martínez, Mexico, Cultura, 1919. *Obras completas*, 29 vols., Madrid, Biblioteca Nueva, 1920–1928; edited by Alfonso Reyes.

TRANSLATIONS: Blackwell, 34–67. Craig, 76–87. Kress, Dorothy, *Confessions of a Modern Poet*, Boston, 1935. Rice, W. F., *Plenitude*, Los Angeles, 1928. Teja Zabre, A., *Plenitude*, Mexico, 1938. Underwood, 59–65. Walsh, *Cath. Anth.*, 370–371. Walsh, *Hisp. Anth.*, 626–634.

CRITICAL REFERENCES: •Blanco-Fombona, *El modernismo*, 253–273. Goldberg, 75–81. González Peña, 233–236. "Lauxar," 199–212. •*Nosotros*, "Homenaje a Amado Nervo," June, 1919. Onís, 396–399 and 1185; extensive bibliography. Oyuela, III, vol. 2, 955–968. •Reyes, Alfonso, *Tránsito de Amado Nervo*, Santiago de Chile, Ercilla, 1937. •Wellman, Esther Turner, *Amado Nervo, Mexico's Religious Poet*, New York, Instituto de las Españas, 1936.

** f. (PERU) **José Santos Chocano** (1875–1934), first among Peruvian modernists, was at various times in his life a revolutionary, a picaresque criminal who became involved in many love intrigues, a hectic nationalist, and a political prisoner. In his poetry, Chocano was all this plus a defender of the Indian, an exalter of Spain, a seeker of Spanish-Indian amalgamation and unity, and a champion of revolt against North American imperialism. As a painter of tropic loveliness and the lush seductive color and strength of that great zone he is unexcelled. His verse is at times bombastic, wordy, worthless, and irritating, but at others it is simple, spontaneous, touchingly beautiful. Chocano gave an "indianista" slant to modernism. He was shot to death while riding in a streetcar in Chile.

SUGGESTED READING: "La epopeya del Pacífico," "Blasón," "Caupolicán," "Cuathemoc," "Ollantá," "El sueño del caimán," "Tres notas de nuestra alma indígena," and other poems.

TEXTS: Coester, *Anthology*, 179–207. Onís, 427–444. Torres-Ríoseco, *Antología*, 188–190.

EDITIONS: *Alma América*, Madrid, 1906. *Fiat Lux*, Paris, 1908; study by A. González Blanco. *Poesías completas*, Barcelona, 1910. *Primicias de oro de Indias*, Santiago de Chile, 1934. *Poesías escogidas*, Paris, 1938 (Biblioteca de cultura peruana, 12).

TRANSLATIONS: Blackwell, 206–229. Craig, 130–145. Underwood, Edna W., *Spirit of the Andes*, Portland, 1935.

CRITICAL REFERENCES: •Blanco-Fombona, *El modernismo*, 273–295. Cejador y Frauca, X, 284–289. García Calderón, *Del romanticismo*, 210–218. García Calderón, *Semblanzas*, 104–124. •Goldberg, 246–295. "Lauxar," 213–226. •Meza Fuentes, Roberto, "La poesía de José Santos Chocano," *Nosotros*, April-December, 1934, 286–311. Onís, 427–429 and 1186; extensive bibliography. Santos González, 509–540; essays by M. G. Prada and V. García Calderón. Umphrey, G. W., "José Santos Chocano," *Hispania*, III (1920), 304–315.

*   g. (URUGUAY) **Julio Herrera y Reissig** (1875–1910) was the extremely sensitive son of an illustrious family fallen into disgrace. Books and literature were his life, and he never left the country

of his birth. He founded a literary group of Bohemian poets, called the "Torre de los Panoramas," which met in the attic of his father's house. Herrera y Reissig was fervently admired by this small clique, and his superiority soon burned him out. His poetry ranges from simple lyricism to extreme complexity. He is the outstanding symbolist of the "modernista" group, links modernism to ultraism,[4] and is distinctly a poet for the fit though few. His work was produced between 1900 and 1910 and was dispersed in periodicals; it was not collected until after his death.

SUGGESTED READING: "Desolación absurda," "Julio," "El cura," "Nirvana crepuscular," "La sombra dolorosa," and other poems.

TEXTS: Coester, *Anthology,* 160–166. Holmes, *Span. Am.,* 459–461. Onís, 469–488. Oyuela, III, vol. 2, 637–640. Torres-Ríoseco, *Antología,* 192–193.

EDITIONS: *Obras completas,* 5 vols., Montevideo, 1913. *Prosas, crítica, cuentos, comentarios,* prologue by V. A. Salaverri, Montevideo, 1918. *Los parques abandonados,* Montevideo, 1919. *Páginas escogidas,* preliminary study by J. Mas y Pi, Barcelona, 1919. *Antología lírica,* compiled by C. Sabat Ercasty and Manuel de Castro, containing a study and bibliography, Santiago, 1939.

TRANSLATIONS: Blackwell, 444–445. Craig, 126–129. Walsh, *Cath. Anth.,* 396–397. Walsh, *Hisp. Anth.,* 683–686.

CRITICAL REFERENCES: •Blanco-Fombona, *El modernismo,* 191–221. García Calderón, *Semblanzas,* 77–90. "Lauxar," 397–444. Onís, 469–472 and 1187; extensive bibliography. Zum Felde, *Crítica,* 201–215. •Zum Felde, *Proceso,* II, 115–150.

---

[4] The Hispanic term for a sort of new gongorism whose excesses held a brief but powerful sway in the 1920's. Most of the so-called "ultraístas" and "vanguardistas" soon outgrew the fad and in fuller maturity found a more moderate perspective. Such movements do not generally appeal to the layman who reads poetry only on occasion, but poets themselves are frequently fired by the worship of some new fetish (or some old fetish in new garb), and such cults often help them to achieve a finer poetic sensitivity, a fresher language.

*

**h.** (MEXICO) **Enrique González Martínez** (1871– ), practiced medicine in the Mexican provinces for seventeen years, went to Mexico City in 1911, where he held several professorial and political positions, and later became Mexican Minister to Argentina and Spain. Both his life and works are marked by an innate serenity. His poetry is serious, sensitive, terse, sometimes ironic, always carefully wrought. It expresses the reaction against the "modernista" worship of cold marble and graceful swans, sets up the owl instead, and wants to wring the neck of the deceptively plumaged swan.

SUGGESTED READING: "Irás sobre la vida de las cosas," "Como hermana y hermano," "Tuércele el cuello al cisne . . . ," "Mañana los poetas . . . ," "Viento sagrado," "Psalle et sile," "Dolor, si por acaso . . . ," and other poems.

TEXTS: Coester, *Anthology,* 208–210. Holmes, *Span. Am.,* 375–376. Onís, 488–503.

EDITIONS: *Preludios,* Mazatlán, 1903. *Los senderos ocultos,* Mocorito, 1911; Mexico, 1915. *La muerte del cisne,* Mexico, 1915. *Jardines de Francia,* versiones de poetas franceses contemporáneos, prologue by P. Henríquez Ureña, Mexico, 1915, 1919. *Los cien mejores poemas de Enrique González Martínez,* with a study by M. Toussaint, Mexico, 1920. *El romero alucinado,* critical note by E. Díez-Canedo, Buenos Aires, 1923. *Poesías,* 3 vols., Mexico, 1938–1940; carefully corrected by the author.

TRANSLATIONS: Blackwell, 100–108. Craig, 146–153. Underwood, 46–56.

CRITICAL REFERENCES: •Blanco-Fombona, *El modernismo,* 351–355. •Díez-Canedo, Enrique, "Enrique González Martínez en su plenitud," *Revista iberoamericana,* II (1940), 383–389. Goldberg, 82–92. González Peña, 237–238. Onís, 488–490 and 1187; extensive bibliography. Reyes, Alfonso, introductory study to *Los senderos ocultos,* Mexico, 1915.

3. The modernist novel.

General characteristics: more or less the same as those of modernist poetry; careful avoidance of the social or economic problems close at hand; touches of poetry, fantasy, exoticism, philosophy, highly stylized language, wishful thinking; interesting as an art form rather than enlightening presentation of an epoch.

\* (VENEZUELA) **Manuel Díaz Rodríguez** (1868–1927), the most famous Venezuelan modernist, traveled extensively in Italy and France and was well acquainted with European literature. His lyrical *Cuentos de color* appeared in *El cojo ilustrado* in and around 1898, and were soon reproduced in French translation in Paris. The style of these and of Díaz Rodríguez's later works suggest a carefully laid mosaic of high polish and many blended colors. The central theme is generally the author's sense of artistic frustration in contact with a world which does not understand.

SUGGESTED READING: *Sangre patricia.*

TEXTS AND EDITIONS: *Idolos rotos,* Paris, 1901. *Idolos rotos,* Madrid, 1919. *Sangre patricia,* Caracas, 1902; the best brief example of the "modernista" novel; the Madrid 1916 edition also contains *Cuentos de color. Camino de perfección,* Caracas, 1907; essay and companion piece to *Ariel* of Rodó. *Peregrina o El pozo encantado, novela de rústicos del valle de Caracas,* Madrid, 1922; also contains three short stories.

CRITICAL REFERENCES: Blanco-Fombona, *Letras y letrados,* 233–235. •Ratcliff, 175–189. •Torres-Ríoseco, *Novelistas contemp.,* 353–378.

4. The modernist essay.

General characteristics: a desire to enlighten and better Spanish American thought and action. However, the style of writing varies with each author, running the gamut of expression from González Prada's diatribes to Rodó's long-sentenced and overpolished paragraphs replete with literary allusions and semiphilosophical thought.

* **a.** (PERU) **Manuel González Prada** (1844–1918), inheritor of the mantle of the Ecuadorean Juan Montalvo, and wielder of choice invective, was born an aristocrat but became Peru's most dynamic, combative champion of the underdog, and the principal wayclearer for its social reform movement, "Aprismo."[5] As a child González Prada ran away from the seminary where he had been sent to study, and in early maturity (but only after his religious mother's death) he began to hurl attacks at the Catholic Church. For several years he held a position as head of the national library, and was active in politics throughout his life. Despite scabrous phrases and pregnant diatribe, his style is cut with the precision of a lapidary. He preached national union, hatred of the Lima bureaucracy, defense of the Indians, and repression of the clerical oligarchy. In order to unleash this ceaseless propaganda of attack, he founded several journals, collaborated on many others, and accepted exile and enmity with apparent relish. He attempted to perform an autopsy on Peru's festering social, economic, and religious system. His viewpoint is summed up in his battle cry: "¡Los viejos a la tumba, los jóvenes a la obra!" He modeled the mentality of succeeding socialist-aprista generations (José Carlos Mariátegui, Raúl Haya de la Torre, Luis Alberto Sánchez, etc.). Many of González Prada's works have only recently been assembled and published posthumously in book form by his son. They prove him to be a fine poet, particularly of ironic verse, as well as Spanish America's most colorful essayist.

SUGGESTED READING: Among his poems "Triolets" and "Rondeles" from the *Antología*, "Buen amor," "Cura y corregidor,"

---

[5] The pro-Indian, antiforeign, semisocialistic political and social movement founded in 1923 by Haya de la Torre. It is a tremendous and growing force in Peru, Bolivia, and Ecuador today, and is largely responsible for the Indian reforms effected in those countries in the past few years. See *The Other Spanish Christ*, by John A. Mackay (New York, Macmillan, 1932), and *Fire on the Andes*, by Carleton Beals (Philadelphia, Lippincott, 1934).

"Cervantes," and other poems. Among his essays numbers III and IV in the second part of *Nuevas páginas libres,* and other selections.

TEXTS AND EDITIONS: Holmes, *Span. Am.,* 432–433. Onís, 4–5. *Páginas libres,* Paris, 1894; Madrid, 1915. *Horas de lucha,* Lima, 1908. *Bajo el oprobio,* Paris, 1933; prologue by Alfredo González Prada, the author's son. *Nuevas páginas libres,* Santiago, Ercilla, 1937. *Antología poética de Manuel González Prada,* Mexico, Cultura, 1940 (Clásicos de América); introduction by Carlos García Prada.

CRITICAL REFERENCES: •Blanco-Fombona, introductory study in Madrid 1915 edition of *Páginas libres* (see editions above). García Calderón, *Semblanzas,* 175–184. Onís, 3–4 and 1175. •Sánchez, Luis Alberto, *Don Manuel,* Santiago de Chile, Ercilla, 1930.

** **b.** (URUGUAY) **José Enrique Rodó** (1872–1917) was the best-known modernist after Rubén Darío; his classic prose was the envy of all succeeding Spanish American writers. Rodó was educated in Montevideo, where in 1895 he helped found *La revista nacional de literatura y ciencia sociales,* for which he wrote many essays. In 1899 his name was widely heralded when he prefaced the second edition of Darío's *Prosas profanas.* Rodó exerted a tremendous influence on other modernist essayists: Manuel Díaz Rodríguez of Venezuela, Manuel González Prada of Peru, and Carlos Reyles of Uruguay. His first and most famous work, *Ariel,* 1900, is still considered by many to be the ethical Bible of Latin America; it calls for the preservation of an intellectual aristocracy to withstand the materialistic impact of the United States (Caliban), carefully points out the good and bad elements of our civilization, urges that the two Americas co-operate and complement each other. Despite the great acclaim accorded Rodó among his own people, his overwrought, almost declamatory style prevents his being (as many Spanish Americans think he is) as great as Emerson, Montaigne, or Bacon.

SUGGESTED READING: *Ariel.*

TEXTS: Coester, *Anthology,* 148–159. Holmes, *Span. Am.,* 484–488. *Ariel* (ed. Rice), Chicago, Univ. of Chicago Press, [1929]. *Ariel* (ed. Nin-Frías and Fitz-Gerald), New York, Sanborn, 1928. *Ariel,* Santiago de Chile, Ercilla, 1936. Torres-Ríoseco, *Antología,* 129–132.

EDITIONS: *Ariel,* Montevideo, 1900. *Los motivos de Proteo,* Montevideo, 1909. *El mirador de Próspero,* Montevideo, 1914. *Hombres de América,* Montevideo, 1920.

TRANSLATIONS: Stimson, F. J. (trans.), *Ariel,* Boston, Houghton Mifflin, 1922; contains introductory essay on author. Flores, Angel (trans.), *The Motives of Proteus,* New York, Brentano's, 1928; contains brief essay on Rodó by Havelock Ellis.

CRITICAL REFERENCES: Andrade Coello, A., *Rodó,* Quito, 1915. Ezcurra, A. T., "Recuerdos y revisión de Rodó," *Universidad,* Mexico, December, 1937. García Calderón, *Semblanzas,* 7–25. García Godoy, *Americanismo literario,* 73–152. •Goldberg, 184–245. Henríquez Ureña, M., *Rodó y Rubén Darío,* Havana, 1918. "Lauxar," 365–396. •"Lauxar," *Rubén Darío y José Enrique Rodó,* Montevideo, 1924. Pérez Petit, V., *Rodó,* Montevideo, 1919; pp. 495–503 contain extensive bibliography. Zaldumbide, Gonzalo, "José Enrique Rodó," Madrid, Editorial-América, 1919 (Biblioteca Andrés Bello, LXII).

**c. (VENEZUELA) Manuel Díaz Rodríguez (1868–1927).**

EDITION: *Camino de perfección,* Caracas, 1907.

See Section D, III, 3.

## IV. Realism.

1. Novelists and short-story writers.

General characteristics: headlong flight from the ivory tower into the midst of local environments; their subjects range from life in Buenos Aires to crude "rioplatense" gauchos, Chilean miners, small-town types from the Mexican countryside. In the novel we find a plethora of local terms, windy moralizations, a style that is lengthy but vigorous. The short stories and sketches may be similarly characterized but in reduced focus; they depend almost entirely on milieu descriptions and broadly drawn character types. Development is often primitive, but there are occasional examples of considerable merit.

a. (MEXICO) **José López-Portillo y Rojas** (1850–1923) was born in Guadalajara of a prominent family; he studied law in Mexico City and later became a distinguished professor of that subject. During his life he traveled widely in England, France, Italy, and the Orient, and acquired an extensive culture, which included a profound knowledge of French, English, and Spanish literatures. He held the governorship of Jalisco and other important political posts. Besides novels, López-Portillo y Rojas wrote some poetry, drama, travel sketches, criticism, and history.

SUGGESTED READING: *La parcela* (selections).

TEXTS AND EDITIONS: Torres-Ríoseco and Sims, 51–65. *La parcela,* Mexico, Agüeros, 1898. *Novelas cortas,* Mexico, Agüeros, 1900. *Los precursores,* Mexico, Agüeros, 1909. *Fuertes y débiles,* Mexico, Libería Española, [1919].

CRITICAL REFERENCES: Carreño, Alberto María, *El licenciado José López-Portillo y Rojas,* Mexico, 1923. •González Peña, 248–249. Iguíniz, 192–197. Starr, 313–333; contains many excerpts translated into English.

b. (MEXICO) **Federico Gamboa** (1864–1939) stands apart from the above-mentioned Mexican realists in his tendency to naturalism and his obsession with the emotional (pathological) conflicts of city life. He felt a strong admiration for the French Zola and the Goncourts, but this feeling was punctuated with a frequent religious sentiment. Gamboa was born in Mexico City, where his family early suffered adverse fortune. Hardship sharpened the author's sensibilities and helped him to self-made manhood. He led a very successful diplomatic and literary career. Gamboa left four Zolaesque, sermon-filled novels of social reform, one on religious salvation, and several dramas. In later life he taught Mexican literature in the National University, and was President of the Mexican Academy of Letters.

SUGGESTED READING: *Santa* (selections).

EDITIONS: *Suprema ley,* Paris and Mexico, Bouret, 1896. *Metamorfosis,* Mexico, Centro Mercantil, 1899. *Santa,* Barcelona, Araluce, 1903. *Reconquista,* Mexico and Barcelona, Gómez de la Puente, 1908. *La llaga,* Mexico, Gómez de la Puente, [1912].

CRITICAL REFERENCES: Cejador y Frauca, X, 163 and 165. Gamboa, Federico, *Mi diario, mucho de mi vida y algo de la de otros,* Mexico, 1907–1938. •González Peña, 252–253. Iguíniz, 141–146. Moore, Ernest, "Bibliografía de obras y crítica de Federico Gamboa," *Revista iberoamericana,* II (1940), 270–279. Starr, 405–420; contains many excerpts translated into English.

c. (ARGENTINA) **Carlos María Ocantos** (1860– ) claims to have initiated the "novela galdosiana" in his country; he has been called the "patriarch of Argentine letters" and also the "Balzac of Argentina." Both claims are only superficially true. Ocantos is often prolix, and oftentimes his characters are weakly delineated, his plots almost ridiculous; his passages on customs and daily life are generally good. The author lived most of his life in Spain separated from the main currents of Argentine literature; he was elected a member of the Spanish Royal Academy.

SUGGESTED READING: *León Zaldívar.*

TEXT: *León Zaldívar* (ed. Rice), New York, Crofts, 1937.

EDITIONS: *León Zaldívar,* Madrid, Imp. de Fortanet, 1888. *Don Perfecto,* Barcelona, Montaner y Simón, 1902.

CRITICAL REFERENCES: •Andersson, Theodore, *Carlos María Ocantos, Argentine Novelist,* Yale Univ. Press, 1934. Cejador y Frauca, X, 132 and 138–139.

d. (URUGUAY) **Eduardo Acevedo Díaz** (1851–1924) was one of the first good novelists of the so-called "mester de gauchería." His work inaugurated and closed the epoch of the historical novel in Uruguay and stimulated gaucho prose in the entire River Plate region. Acevedo Díaz studied law, fought in the revolutionary army, engaged in politics and journalism, held several diplomatic posts, was twice exiled, and in 1903 fled from Uruguay never to return. His entire work was written in exile. His style was naturalistic on the whole, but there were passages of romance and characters symbolic of his country's principal types. His first three novels were a nationalistic trilogy called a "hymn to blood"; his last and briefest novel, *Soledad,* 1894, became a model for later gauchesque prose.

SUGGESTED READING: *Soledad.*

EDITIONS: *Ismael,* Buenos Aires, 1888. *Nativa,* Montevideo, 1890. *Grito de gloria,* Montevideo, 1894. *Soledad,* Montevideo, 1894. *Soledad,* Montevideo, 1931.

CRITICAL REFERENCES: Lasplaces, Alberto, preface to *Soledad,* 1931 (see above editions). Torres-Ríoseco, *Novela,* 213–214. •Zum Felde, *Proceso,* I, 275–307.

e. (PERU) **Clorinda Matto de Turner** (1854–1909), wife of an English doctor, wrote one of the first "indianista" novels depicting the lives of the exploited natives in Peru, where approximately 65 per cent of the population is pure Indian. Her novel was greeted with many shudders of protest on the part of the large landowners, but cleared the way for later works defending the Indians and anathematizing their white masters—works which loom large on the literary horizon of Peru, Ecuador, Bolivia, and Mexico in the twentieth century.

SUGGESTED READING: *Aves sin nido,* Chaps. XXVI–XXX.

EDITION: *Aves sin nido,* Valencia, Madrid, Barcelona, Sempere y Compañía, 1889; with a prologue on the author by Emilio Gutiérrez de Quintanilla.

CRITICAL REFERENCES: Meléndez, 171–178. Sosa, Francisco, *Escritores y poetas sud-americanos,* Mexico, Tip. de la Secretaría de Fomento, 1890, 181–208.

f. (ARGENTINA) **Martiniano P. Leguizamón** (1858–1935), born in the province of Entre Ríos, became a professor of literature and history in Buenos Aires. His many fine naturalistic, regional, gauchesque short stories and sketches and his drama *Calandria* (1896) had a revitalizing effect on Argentine prose and served to perpetuate all that was national in the gaucho literature which had gone before. Leguizamón was also an excellent critic and historian of the gaucho epoch.

SUGGESTED READING: "El forastero" and "El tiro de gracia."

TEXT: García Calderón, *Cuentos,* 85–92 and 179–186.

EDITIONS: *Calandria,* comedia, Buenos Aires, 1896. *Recuerdos de la tierra,* precedidos de una introducción por Joaquín V. González, Buenos Aires, F. Lajouane, 1896. *Alma nativa,* Buenos Aires, 1906. *De cepa criolla,* La Plata, 1908. *Páginas argentinas,* crítica literaria e histórica, Buenos Aires, 1911. *Montaraz,* novela, Buenos Aires, 1911.

TRANSLATION: *Calandria, A Drama of Gaucho Life,* New York, [Hispanic Society], 1932.

CRITICAL REFERENCES: Giusti, Roberto F., "El drama rural argentino," *Nosotros,* V [2nd series] (1937), 241–264. González, Joaquín V., "Introducción" to *Recuerdos de la tierra,* 1896 (see editions above). •Torre Revello, José, *Martiniano Leguizamón, el hombre y su obra* (Museo de Entre Ríos, conferencias de su ciclo 1939), Paraná, 1939.

g. (ARGENTINA) **Roberto J. Payró** (1867–1928) was a journalist, traveler, translator of Zola, writer of "costumbrista" sketches, and dramatist of the contemporary scene. In 1896 he became secretary of the first Center of Socialist Studies in Argentina, of which Leopoldo Lugones and José Ingenieros were also members. He was caught in Belgium during the First World War, where he was imprisoned as an enemy spy after he had expressed bitter hatred of German militarism. His later writings were permeated with these war experiences. Earlier sketches of the Argentine scene are his best; he also left several plays based on social-moral conflicts in Argentine life, of which *Sobre las ruinas* and *Vivir quiero conmigo* are excellent. Journalistic style weakens many of his literary efforts; his masterpiece is *El casamiento de Laucha* (1906), a picaresque novelette.

SUGGESTED READING: *El casamiento de Laucha.*

EDITIONS: *El casamiento de Laucha* (novela picaresca), Buenos Aires, 1906. *El casamiento de Laucha, Chamijo, El falso Inca,* Buenos Aires, Losada, [1940]. *Historia de Pago Chico* (costumbres criollas), Buenos Aires, M. Rodríguez Giles, 1908. *Violines y toneles* (cuentos), Buenos Aires, M. Rodríguez Giles, 1908. *Las divertidas aventuras del nieto de Juan Moreira* (novela), Barcelona, Maucci, n.d. *Teatro: Vivir quiero conmigo* ..., *Fuego en el rastrojo, Mientraiga,* Buenos Aires, Jesús Menéndez, 1925.

TRANSLATIONS: Brenner, A. (trans.), "The Marriage of Laucha" and "The Devil in Pago Chico" in Frank, 1–77, 155–178.

CRITICAL REFERENCES: Estrella Gutiérrez and Suárez Calimano, 349–354. Giusti, Roberto F., "La obra literaria de Roberto Payró" in *Las divertidas aventuras del nieto de Juan Moreira* (see editions above).  •Larra, Raúl, *Payró, el hombre y la obra,* Buenos Aires, Claridad, [1938].  •*Nosotros,* May, 1928, "Homenaje a Roberto J. Payró."

**      h. (CHILE) **Baldomero Lillo** (1867–1923) was the first Chilean short-story writer to accentuate the social problems of his country's national life. He was born of a middle-class family, and as a child heard his father relate mining experiences which he had gone through in several parts of Chile and in the state of California, U.S.A. The son, Baldomero, was employed by a Chilean mining company, and finally became manager of the company store. He read voluminously (French and Russian naturalism, especially), and Zola's *Germinal* left a deep imprint on his work. In 1898 he went to Santiago, where he immediately identified himself with the problems of the city workers, and often attended "tertulias" frequented by a group of his brother's friends known as the "generación de novecientos." He secured a position in the section of publications of the University of Chile. In 1917 he had to give up this university work because of ill health, and from that time until his death he received a pension from the national government. He left only two first-rate works, *Sub terra* (1904) and *Sub sole* (1907).

SUGGESTED READING:  "El chiflón del diablo" or "El pago."

TEXTS:  *Hispanoamericanos* (ed. Jones and Hansen), New York, Holt, 1941, 173–186.  Torres-Ríoseco and Kress, 95–106.

EDITION:  *Sub sole,* Santiago, Nascimento, 1931; contains a study on Lillo by González Vera, 195–264.

CRITICAL REFERENCES:  See edition above. Sedgwick, Ruth, "El mensaje social de Baldomero Lillo," *Memoria del Segundo Congreso Internacional de Catedráticos de Literatura Iberoamericana,* Mexico, 1941. Silva Castro, Raúl, *Los cuentistas chilenos,* Santiago, 1937, 229–241.

**2. The Theater.**

General characteristics: realistic drama of merit is produced only in the "rioplatense" region during the period 1888–1910. It is generally gauchesque or rustic in character. Highly regarded Florencio Sánchez, who cleared the way for this type of theater, may seem primitive to modern readers; later dramatists like Roberto J. Payró, who are not so important, are easier and more enjoyable to read.

** **a.** (URUGUAY) **Florencio Sánchez** (1875–1910), claimed by both Argentina and Uruguay, was the principal founder and master proponent of the "teatro rioplatense." He was born in Montevideo of a middle-class family, and in that city held several minor journalistic and governmental positions, although he was generally at odds with his employer because of his radical views. Participation in the revolution of 1896–1897 cured him of political idealism. He drank heavily, wrote hurriedly (often on the backs of telegraph pads in smoke-reeking rooms), and seldom revised.

Florencio Sánchez produced twenty plays within six years (1903–1909). In 1910 he was sent to Italy on a visit made possible by a slim and tardy financial subsidy of the Uruguayan government but died shortly after his arrival. His drama is of three general types—rural, urban, thesis—but the three are often intermingled. He has been called by some critics "el Ibsen criollo," but he lacks the careful, consummate, and universal artistry of the great Scandinavian playwright. His importance is great, but it is mainly historic and does not enter into the main currents of world literature. Unlike Ibsen, Florencio Sánchez marks the beginning rather than the culmination of a theatrical tradition. None the less he is Spanish America's greatest dramatist; in fact, he is the only Spanish American playwright who has gained any notable recognition throughout the entire region. The dates of his most important plays are:

*M'hijo el dotor,* 1903; *La gringa,* 1904; *Barranca abajo,* 1905; *Los muertos,* 1905.

SUGGESTED READING: *La gringa.*

TEXT: *La gringa* (ed. Richardson and Lister), New York, Crofts, 1927.

EDITION: *El teatro del uruguayo Florencio Sánchez,* 3 vols., edited with an introductory study by V. A. Salaverri, Buenos Aires, 1920; Barcelona, 1926.

CRITICAL REFERENCES: Estrella Gutiérrez and Suárez Calimano, 407–412. Giusti, Roberto F., *Florencio Sánchez, su vida y su obra,* Buenos Aires, 1920. •Richardson, Ruth, *Florencio Sánchez and the Argentine Theater,* New York, Instituto de las Españas, 1923. Vázquez Cey, Arturo, *Florencio Sánchez y el teatro argentino,* Buenos Aires, 1929. Zum Felde, *Crítica,* 219–232.

b. (ARGENTINA) **Roberto J. Payró** (1867–1928). The dates of his plays are: *Canción trágica,* 1900; *Sobre las ruinas,* 1904; *Vivir quiero conmigo,* 1913. See Section D, IV, 1, g. For Argentine drama in English translation consult *Three Plays of the Argentine,* edited by E. H. Bierstadt, New York, Duffield, 1920. The translator is Jacob S. Fassett.

# The Contemporary Period (1910–1941)

## BY JOHN E. ENGLEKIRK

## INTRODUCTORY SUMMARY

Modernism served to freshen and to vitalize the literary atmosphere of Spanish America, clearing it of the lingering gossamers of colonial thought and sweeping away many of the hackneyed expressions of a chronic romanticism. Its benefits were many, as we have seen already, but its stress on form and its aristocratic cosmopolitan leanings soon lured the weaker of its disciples into the void of barren artificiality. That which but a short time before had been original and promising in its turn became hackneyed and sterile in the hands of those who betrayed their American heritage and remained indifferent to the mounting social and political challenges of the opening years of the century. The Spanish-American War, the growing threat of "Yankee" hegemony, impending social revolt, and the increasingly stronger influence exerted by French, Spanish, and Russian realists and naturalists brought about a reaction, however, against the escapist attitude of the modernists and their extravagant devotion to form and beauty. This reaction had definitely asserted itself by 1911, the year when Enrique González Martínez wrote his famous sonnet entitled "Tuércele el cuello al cisne...," in which he decried the empty ritualism of the "rubendarianos" and at the same time welcomed the sincere, more meaningful poetry of the postmodernist group. "Art for art's sake" no longer held any appeal for a generation alive to the need for serious thought and purposeful action. Thinking men everywhere sought to define and to interpret the American scene and to ponder the immediate specific problems of their time.

The period opens with the Mexican Revolution of 1910, the first significant movement for social and economic reform in America—all other revolutionary attempts of the past having been fundamentally and almost exclusively political, the attempt of the ousted to regain control. The submerged masses—the Indian, the laborer, "los de abajo" in general—soon became the theme of those writers who sought to document and to give impetus to the conflict that spread in varying degrees throughout most of Spanish America. Literati everywhere took up the fight for reform, exposing and denouncing injustice and tyranny and championing the cause of the "forgotten man," regardless of his race—Indian, Negro, or mestizo—or of his origin—Amazon jungle, Venezuelan "llanos," Andean plateau, or festering urban centers. Literature was brought down out of the "ivory tower" of the modernists to record the social trends of the day. Even the so-called "novela indianista" cast off the romantic coloring of its past to join the family of the starkly realistic, proletarian-type novel of the last decade.

The First World War, too, exerted a direct influence on the course of Spanish American letters and thought. Rapidly expanding trade and soaring foreign investments—largely from the United States, which poured postwar millions into her sister nations' coffers with no concern over their ability to pay—ushered in a period of economic prosperity and political corruption that only drew to a close in 1929 when the world-wide debacle spread depression and accelerated sociopolitical revolt over all Ibero-America. The European conflict brought Spanish America and Anglo-America into even closer economic and political relations. At the outset, the insistence of the United States on a unilateral interpretation of hemispheric policy served as an additional goad to prod Spanish American nations to lay aside feuds and differences among themselves in order to present a more effective front to this "Yankee" threat. The most determined resistance took shape in the form of a strong anti-imperialistic movement known as "aprismo" (APRA–Alianza Popular Revolucionaria Americana) that sprang up in Peru in the twenties to combat not only "Yankee" but all foreign hegemony of whatever origin and to launch a youth reform crusade under the nativist banners of Indo-America. On the other hand, however, the surge of racial sympathy that her former colonies experienced after her defeat in 1898 drew Spain—spiritually and culturally—more deeply than ever before within the sisterhood of Hispanic nations, a rapprochement that gained in intensity as the ideological cleavage in the motherland became more acute with the founding of the Second Republic in 1931. Pan-Hispanism, Indo-Americanism, and Pan-Americanism—since the inauguration of the good-neighbor policy in 1932, this last movement bids fair for the first time to take on a vital meaning in Spanish America—are among the more important currents of this period that run counter to the rising wave of ardent nationalism that characterizes much of the literature of recent years. These conflicting ideologies are indicative of an America that is rapidly approaching maturity; they give direction to the course that is being pursued in the solution of the multiple problems, social, political, and economic, confronting twentieth-century Spanish America. These forces and trends and problems constitute the very essence of contemporary literature and thought.

It was to be expected, therefore, that prose should have become the more important medium of expression since 1910. The essay reveals the intense intellectual activity of present-day America; the short story and the novel are focused sharply on the American scene. Poetry, on the other hand, still appears to be seeking a path more in consonance with the new American spirit: no great poet has yet appeared in the last thirty years to lead the way or to challenge the supremacy of the modernists. The theater, groping and sporadic in the past, has suffered heavily since the advent of the motion picture. No one figure stands out since the days of the Uruguayan dramatist Florencio Sánchez, and for the purposes of the survey it is not essential that any study be made of certain relatively minor events that characterize the development of the theater since 1910—in Mexico: Teatro de Ulises (1929), Teatro de Ahora (1932), Teatro de Orientación (1933); in Chile: social-reform dramas of Alejandro Flores's Compañía Nacional de Comedias of the thirties; in Argentina: Teatro del Pueblo, under the guidance of Leónidas Barletta since the early thirties. In the capitals of the Río de la Plata countries alone can there be said to exist something like a national theater where nativist tendencies, historical plots, and themes of social conflict have enriched the budding dramatic tradition of the early years of the present century.

Foreign literary trends no longer dominate the American scene, nor are France and Spain the sole arbiters of America's literary destiny. Paris has ceased to be the Mecca of the Spanish American artist, and the Spanish-Indian heritage has regained its rightful place in the cultural life of America. Traditional themes and popular forms have supplanted the exotic note and experimental metrics of the modernists. Gallicisms have surrendered the field in the face of a veritable barrage of regionalisms. Americans everywhere are bent on creating an original literary art, divorced in language, in theme, and in spirit as completely as possible from the European models they have been accused of imitating in servile fashion ever since political independence was won. It is true, of course, that several of the innumerable postwar isms of Europe found their way to America, brought here in fact by the very men who helped bring them into being: Vicente Huidobro of Chile and Jorge Luis Borges of Argentina. "Creacionismo" and "ultraísmo" are the names by which these ultraradical, ephemeral movements of the twenties are still vaguely remembered in the Hispanic world of today. But it should likewise be noted that in keeping with the heightened racial sympathy that marked the attitude of Spanish America toward Spain before the civil war, these postwar currents reached America largely through the mother country rather than directly and exclusively from France. Then, too, as if grateful to the modernists for having revealed to her a new aesthetic world, renascent Spain repaid her debt to America through the inspiration which the postmodernists received from the poetry of Juan Ramón Jiménez and Federico García Lorca, to cite but two of the most illustrious and most representative poets of Spain whose influence on American letters since the First World War has far outshadowed that of a Paul Valéry or Apollinaire of France or that of the revolutionary Whitman. Contemporary prose writers have not been altogether free of the inescapable influence of certain world-famous novelists, of Joyce, of Proust, of Romains; and the imitation of

French realists and naturalists and of the Russians, although no longer so pronounced as in their earlier period, is still discernible in many of their more recent works.

The modernist period witnessed a veritable flowering of the literary review as the herald of the new aesthetics (see Section D, Introductory Summary). This new review was continental and international in spirit and in theme, in refreshing contrast to the lifeless, local tone of its predecessor. After 1910, three relatively distinct types appeared to take its place: (1) one that, like it, served as the mouthpiece for the more recent literary currents and schools; (2) one that was continental in scope but no longer the organ of any one literary movement; and (3) one that was devoted almost exclusively to national letters and in many instances to other aspects of cultural life as well. The journals of the first type have been even more short-lived as a class than many of those of the modernist period. Among the more ephemeral ones may be cited two of the better known "ultraísta" reviews of Buenos Aires—*Proa* (1921) and *Prisma* (1921). The pro-Indian movement in Peru gave birth to the historical *Amauta* (Lima, 1926–1930), while the younger Mexican group contributed the excellent *Contemporáneos* (Mexico, 1928–1931). The second type claims several of the oldest and most significant of the current journals of contemporary America: *Nosotros* (Buenos Aires, 1907– ); *Repertorio americano* (San José, C.R., 1919– ); *América* (Quito, 1924– ); and *Atenea* (Concepción, Chile, 1924– ). To this group should be added such recent reviews as *Revista hispánica moderna* (New York, 1934– ), *Revista iberoamericana* (Mexico, 1939– ), and *Revista de filología hispánica* (Buenos Aires, 1939– ), which even though not entirely Spanish American in origin may be classed among the best in the field of Spanish American bibliography, literary criticism, and language. Closely rivaling this second group in quality and importance and far surpassing it in numbers is that of the national literary reviews, of which only a few may be listed here: *Revista bimestre cubana* (Habana, second period, 1910– ); *Cuba contemporánea* (Habana, 1913–1927); *Cultura venezolana* (Caracas, 1918–1931); *El libro y el pueblo* (Mexico, 1920–1934); and *Revista nacional de cultura* (Caracas, 1938– ).

General References: Daireaux, Max, *Panorama de la littérature hispanoaméricaine,* Paris, Kra, 1930. Jones, C. K., "Modern Hispanic American Literary Development," in Wilgus, *Mod. Hisp. Am.,* Chap. XIV. Marinello, Juan, *Literatura hispanoamericana,* México, Universidad Nacional, 1937. Onís, xviii–xxiv. Sánchez, *Hist. de la lit. am.,* 476–646. Suárez Calimano, E., "Orientaciones de la literatura hispanoamericana en los últimos veinte años," *Nosotros,* LVII (1927), 285–314. Torres-Ríoseco, *Novela,* 165–171.

## I. Historical background.

1. The Mexican Revolution.
   Fall of the Díaz regime (May 25, 1911).
   The "war" years (1911–1917).
   Adoption of the new Mexican constitution (May 1, 1917).
   Cárdenas and the Six-Year Plan (1934–1940).
   REFERENCES: Gruening, Ernest, *Mexico and Its Heritage,* New York, Century, 1928, 91–108, 141–167, 211–390, 515–530, 635–664. Tannenbaum, Frank, *Peace by Revolution,* New York, Columbia Univ. Press, 1933, Chaps. XI–XXVI.

2. Other movements of political, economic, and social change.
   Advanced political, social, and economic reforms in Uruguay (1911–1927).
   Electoral reforms in Argentina (1912).
   Arturo Alessandri, "first president of the Chilean *people,*" elected 1920.
   APRA (Alianza Popular Revolucionaria Americana) founded by Haya de la Torre in Peru in 1923.
   REFERENCES: Rippy, Chap. XIII. Wilgus, *Mod. Hisp. Am.,* Chap. X.

3. Dictatorships, depression, and internal strife.
   Leguía, despot of Peru (1919–1930).

Estrada Cabrera, dictator of Guatemala (1898–1920).

Juan Vicente Gómez, dictator of Venezuela (1908–1935).

Serious military uprisings in Paraguay (1920–1924).

REFERENCE: Rippy, Chap. XIV.

4. Inter-American and Pan-American relations.

Pan-American Conferences: fourth at Buenos Aires in 1910; fifth at Santiago, Chile, in 1923; sixth at Havana in 1928; seventh at Montevideo in 1933; and eighth at Lima in 1938.

United States marines and intervention in Nicaragua (1912, 1916–1932), Santo Domingo (1914–1924), Cuba (1917, 1919–1923), Honduras (1924), and Panama (repeated intervention).

President Roosevelt and the inauguration of the good-neighbor policy (1932).

Abolition of the Platt Amendment, Cuba (1934).

Chaco War between Paraguay and Bolivia (1932–1938).

Inter-American Conference for the Maintenance of Peace, at Buenos Aires (1936).

Inter-American Economic Conference, at Havana (1940).

REFERENCES: Inman, S. G., *Problems in Pan Americanism,* New York, Doran, 1921. Rippy, Chaps. XXIII, XXV. Ugarte, Chaps. IX, XI. See also "Introduction" and "Bibliography" by Rippy for additional items on this section.

II. Important factors influencing contemporary literature.

1. Crosscurrents of New World political thought.
   Pan-Latinism.
   Pan-Hispanism.
   Indo-Americanism.
   Pan-Americanism.
   Rising tide of nationalism.

   REFERENCES: García Calderón, F., 283–289, 298–312, 335–350, 387–400. Haya de la Torre, Víctor Raúl, *¿A dónde va Indoamérica?,*

2d ed., Santiago, Ercilla, 1935. Rippy, Chap. XXI. Ugarte, Chaps. IX–X. Wilgus, *Mod. Hisp. Am.,* Chap. X.

2. The ideology of social revolt.

REFERENCES: García Calderón, F., 351–364. Sánchez, *Hist. de la lit. am.,* 601–608. Torres-Ríoseco, A., "Social Trends in the Latin American Novel," *Quarterly Journal of Inter-American Relations,* I (1939), 76–80. Wilgus, *Mod. Hisp. Am.,* Chaps. IX–X.

3. Foreign literary movements reflected or imitated in Spanish America.

European postwar isms.

Postmodernist literature of Spain: Juan Ramón Jiménez and Federico García Lorca.

Other literary forces: Proust, Joyce, Whitman, etc.

REFERENCES: Borges, Jorge Luis, "Ultraísmo," *Nosotros,* XXXIX (1921), 466–471. Crow, John A., "Federico García Lorca en Hispanoamérica," *Revista iberoamericana,* I (1939), 307–319. Englekirk, John E., "Notes on Whitman in Spanish America," *Hispanic Review,* VI (1938), 133–138. Henríquez Ureña, Max, "Las influencias francesas en la poesía hispanoamericana," *Revista iberoamericana,* II (1940), 401–417. *Indice de la nueva poesía americana,* with prologues by Hidalgo, Huidobro, and Borges, Buenos Aires, 1926.

III. The essay.

The literary artist becomes acutely conscious of his new mission. He rejects the principle of "art for art's sake": he too must aid in the definition and orientation of America. Encompassing the entire gamut of problems confronting America Hispana: political (Ugarte, Blanco-Fombona), racial (Vasconcelos, Fernando Ortiz), historical and cultural (Francisco García Calderón, Ricardo Rojas, Luis Alberto Sánchez), the essay reveals the ideological turmoil of the period. A more studied literary criticism and the widening aesthetic interests of the present generation have likewise made extreme demands on the form. Alfonso Reyes of Mexico has sounded new depths and given added beauty to the essay of his time.

REFERENCES: Carrión, B., *Los creadores de la Nueva América* (Vasconcelos, Ugarte, F. García Calderón, Arguedas, and others), Madrid, Soc. Gen. Esp. de Lib., 1928. Rippy, J. F., *Latin America in World Politics,* New York, Knopf, 1928, 248–253. Sánchez, *Hist. de la lit. am.,* Chap. XVI and 618–623, 625–646.

* 1. (VENEZUELA) **Rufino Blanco-Fombona** (1874– ), officeholder and diplomat and several times a political prisoner during his early years, was forced to seek refuge in Europe, where he has spent much of his life. It was not until after the death of Gómez in 1935 that he returned to his native land. As editor and publisher of his world-famous series of American books (Biblioteca "Andrés Bello," "Ayacucho," etc.), he has contributed much toward making Spanish American literature more widely known. He is one of the most prolific, if not the most objective, literary critics of his generation. His poems and short stories are artistically superior to his novels, most of which passion, satire, and diatribe tend to reduce to the level of polemical journalism. It is, however, as an essayist and a thinker that he has exerted his greatest influence. Even before the turn of the century he began his fiery anti-Yankee campaign, pleading for union against the northern tyrant. He is also one of the most ardent defenders of Spain's role in America and a strong proponent of dynamic Spanish-Americanism.

SUGGESTED READING: Selections from *La lámpara de Aladino, La evolución política y social de Hispanoamérica,* and *El conquistador español del siglo XVI.*

TEXTS: Holmes, *Span. Am.,* 529–532. Onís, 447–460 (poems). Weisinger, 215–229.

EDITIONS: *Cuentos americanos* (1904), Paris, 1913 (Biblioteca moderna ilustrada). *El hombre de hierro* (1907), Madrid, Editorial-

América, [1916]. *La evolución política y social de Hispanoamérica,* Madrid, B. Rodríguez, 1911. *La lámpara de Aladino,* Madrid, Renacimiento, 1915. *El hombre de oro,* Madrid, Editorial-América, [1916]. *El conquistador español del siglo XVI,* Madrid, Mundo Latino, 1922. *El modernismo y los poetas modernistas,* Madrid, Mundo Latino, 1929.

TRANSLATION: Goldberg, Isaac (trans.), *The Man of Gold,* New York, Brentano's, 1920.

CRITICAL REFERENCES: Blanco-Fombona, *Camino de imperfección, diario de mi vida* (1906–1913), Madrid, Editorial-América, [1933]. García Godoy, *La lit. amer.,* 229–244. García Godoy, *Amer. lit.,* 197–244. •Goldberg, 307–359. •Onís, 444–447. Picón-Salas, 199–203. Ratcliff, 145–172.

2. (ARGENTINA) **Manuel Ugarte** (1878– ), militant propagandist, compaigned widely throughout Spanish America in the second decade of this century in an effort to arouse concerted opposition to the growing peril of "Yankee" imperialism of that day. It was he who coined the phrase "el coloso del norte" that Spanish American anti-imperialists have used ever since when referring to the United States. His best creative work has been in the short story—*Cuentos de la Pampa* (1903) and *Cuentos argentinos* (1908), collections that made him famous in France, where he completed his education and where he has spent a good part of his life since 1898. He has also written verse, several novels, and books of travel impressions and literary criticism.

SUGGESTED READING: Selections from *El destino de un continente.*

TEXTS: *Las mejores páginas de Manuel Ugarte,* Barcelona, Araluce, 1929. García Calderón, *Cuentos,* 241–250. Leavitt, vii–xiii, 3–49.

EDITIONS: *El porvenir de la América latina,* Valencia, F. Sempere y Cía., 1911. *El destino de un continente,* Madrid, Mundo Latino, 1923.

TRANSLATION: Phillips, C. A. (trans.), *The Destiny of a Continent,* edited by J. F. Rippy, New York, Knopf, 1925.

CRITICAL REFERENCES: See texts above. •García Godoy, *La lit. amer.,* 61–80, 95–103. Holmes, *Span. Am.,* 65–66. Sánchez, *Hist. de la lit. am.,* 495–496.

** 3. (PERU) **Francisco García Calderón** (1883– ), son of a former president of Peru and brother of the distinguished writer and literary critic Ventura García Calderón, has lived almost continuously in France, where he has represented his country in the diplomatic service for over thirty years. Critic, sociologist, and disciple of Rodó, he is a champion of postmodernist American ideology, interpreting America's problems from the European—specifically Latin—point of view. He is an ardent admirer of France; many of his works are written in the language of that country.

SUGGESTED READING: *Latin America: Its Rise and Progress.* Selections from *La creación de un continente.*

EDITIONS: *Les démocraties latines de l'Amérique,* Paris, Flammarion, 1912. *La creación de un continente,* Paris, Ollendorff, 1913.

TRANSLATION: Miall, B. (trans.), *Latin America: Its Rise and Progress (Les démocraties latines de l'Amérique),* New York, Scribner, 1913.

CRITICAL REFERENCES: •García Godoy, *La. lit. amer.,* 265–281. •García Godoy, *Amer. Lit.,* 153–196. Holmes, *Span. Am.,* 433. •Sánchez, *Hist. de la lit. am.,* 482–483.

* 4. (ARGENTINA) **Ricardo Rojas** (1882– ), one-time professor at the University of La Plata and formerly dean of the Faculty of Philosophy and Letters and rector of the University of Buenos Aires, where he is now professor of national literature (the first to hold such a chair in the Argentine), is an outstanding critic and scholar and a fervent nationalist. As critic and historian of national letters he won the national Grand Prize of Literature in 1921 for his four-

volume work *La literatura argentina*. He has written several volumes of poetry and several historical dramas. His dramatization of the famous Peruvian play *Ollantay* has met with wide acclaim and is unquestionably one of the high points in the history of the modern Spanish American theater. *La argentinidad* and *Eurindia* figure prominently in the list of profound interpretative historical studies of American spirit and culture.

SUGGESTED READING: Selections from *La argentinidad* and *Eurindia*.

TEXTS: Holmes, *Span. Am.,* 46–48 (poems). Noé, 145–152 (poems). Onís, 724–729 (poems).

EDITIONS: *La argentinidad* (1916), 2d ed., Buenos Aires, J. Roldán y Cía., 1922. *Discursos,* Buenos Aires, J. Roldán y Cía., 1924. *Eurindia,* Buenos Aires, J. Roldán y Cía., 1924.

TRANSLATION: Browning, W. E. (trans.), *The Invisible Christ,* New York, The Abingdon Press, 1931.

CRITICAL REFERENCES: See texts above. Sánchez, *Hist. de la lit. am.,* 489–490.

* **5.** (MEXICO) **José Vasconcelos** (1882– ), lawyer, politician, and one-time rector of the University of Mexico, was among the first in America to promulgate revolutionary principles of education for the Indian when called to fill the post of Minister of Public Education under President Obregón from 1920 to 1925. From this latter year on he traveled widely through both Americas, lecturing on contemporary Mexican problems and on racial (*La raza cósmica*) and political (*Bolivarismo y Monroísmo*) questions confronting many countries of the New World. Of his several philosophical studies, *Indología* is especially noteworthy because it represents one of the few attempts yet made by a Spanish American to formulate a New World philosophy. More recently he has told the story of his own stormy existence in a series of four works, the first of which —*Ulises Criollo*—appeared in 1935.

SUGGESTED READING: Selections from *La raza cósmica* and *Indología*.

TEXTS: Holmes, *Span. Am.*, 395–396. Vasconcelos, *Aspects of Mexican Civilization,* Chicago, Univ. of Chicago Press, 1927. *Páginas escogidas,* Mexico, 1940; selection and prologue by Antonio Castro Leal.

EDITIONS: *La raza cósmica,* Paris, Agencia Mundial de Librería, 1925. *Indología* (1927), 2d ed., Barcelona, Agencia Mundial de Librería, [193?]. *Bolivarismo y Monroísmo* (1934), 2d ed., Santiago, Ercilla, 1935. *Ulises Criollo,* 8th ed., Mexico, Botas, 1937.

CRITICAL REFERENCES: See texts above. •González Peña, 287–288. Sánchez, *Hist. de la lit. am.,* 498–499.

6. (MEXICO) **Alfonso Reyes** (1889– ), poet, literary critic, scholar, humanist, and diplomat, was born in Monterrey and received his degree in law from the University of Mexico. From 1913 on he served his country as diplomat in many lands of Europe and America. Much of this time he lived in Spain, where he conceived a deep love and respect for the mother country's great literary masters of the past and won recognition as an authority on Golden Age letters. His own creative work fills many volumes. He is one of America's finest prose stylists and one of her most representative men of universal culture.

SUGGESTED READING: Selections from *Simpatías y diferencias* and *Visión del Anáhuac.*

TEXTS: Holmes, *Span. Am.*, 396–398. Onís, 724–729 (poems). Torres-Ríoseco, *Antología,* 133–136.

EDITIONS: *Visión del Anáhuac* (1917), 2d ed., Madrid, Indice, 1923. *Simpatías y diferencias,* 3 vols., Madrid, Talleres tipográficos del Suc. de E. Teodoro, 1921–1922.

TRANSLATIONS: Underwood, 76, 122–128.

CRITICAL REFERENCES: See texts above. García Godoy, *La lit.*

*amer.*, 247–261.  •González Peña, 288–289.  Sánchez, *Hist. de la lit. am.,* 490–491.

**IV.** Short story and novel.

The weaknesses and defects of the earlier realists and naturalists— poor characterization; wordy, heavy style; excessive attention to detail; lack of perspective; and wearisome moralizations—have been largely overcome by their successors, who have profited aesthetically from the lessons taught them by the modernists and by the more recent revolutionary stylists. The contemporary prose writers in the main defy classification even though critics attempt certain artificial groupings: "novelists of the Mexican Revolution," the "proletarian" school, the "indianista" group, etc.; the common denominator is in most instances America and her people: tropical America, the Andes, Indian America, the Negro, the Creole, America in revolution (social rather than political), but the quotient is richly varied now because of each artist's distinctly personal and critical approach and interpretation. In subject matter, style, and even to a large degree in language, this contemporary fiction is of the New World; and in it one finds for the first time the color, the intensity, the vastness, and the complexity of an America that culturally and spiritually is rapidly coming of age.

REFERENCES: Coester, *Lit. Hist.,* 487–500. Englekirk and Kiddle, *Los de abajo,* New York, Crofts, 1939, xi–lviii. Marinello, 143–165. Onís, "El cuento en América," in Wilkins, vii–xxiv. Ratcliff, Chaps. XIII–XIV. Reid, J. T. "Spanish American Jungle Fiction," *Inter-American Quarterly,* II (1940), 48–58. Sánchez, *Hist. de la lit. am.,* 595–618. Torres-Ríoseco, *Antología,* 26–81. Torres-Ríoseco, *Novela,* 207–243. Torres-Ríoseco, A., "Social Trends in the Latin American Novel," *Quarterly Journal of Inter-American Relations,* I (1939), 76–80. Uslar Pietri, A., "The Spanish American Novel Declares Its Independence," *Books Abroad,* XI (1938), 150–152.

\*    1. (URUGUAY) **Javier de Viana** (1872–1926) was reared on a ranch among gauchos. At the age of eleven he went to Montevideo, where he studied languages and medicine and served a short term in the parliament. In 1904 he became a voluntary exile to Buenos Aires, where he took up journalism, writing articles on the theater. An ardent admirer of nature and a keen observer of men, he became one of the most vigorous regionalists America has produced. His work is extremely somber in tone and is often freighted with local terms and descriptive detail. He stands, however, as the precursor of the best of the contemporary "criollo" school. *Yuyos* and *Leña seca* are among his best collections of short stories.

SUGGESTED READING: Selections from *Leña seca* and from texts recommended below.

TEXTS: Coester, *Cuentos,* 25–31, 59–64. Crow, 171–180. García Calderón, *Cuentos,* 7–26, 92–96, 199–203. Holmes, *Span. Am.,* 478–480. Wilkins, 112–117.

EDITIONS: *Yuyos* (1912), 2d ed., Montevideo, O. M. Bertani, 1912. *Leña seca* (1913), 6th ed., Montevideo, C. García, [192?]. *Gurí y otras novelas,* Madrid, Editorial-América, [1916].

CRITICAL REFERENCES: See texts above. Zum Felde, *Proceso,* II, 193–217.

** 2. (URUGUAY) **Horacio Quiroga** (1878–1937) was born in Salto, Uruguay. At the age of nine he moved to Montevideo, where he lived until 1900. Thereafter, save for a short trip to Paris that same year, he spent the rest of his life in Argentina. After several unsuccessful attempts at making a living from the soil, he turned finally—and with success—to his pen. He is possibly the greatest of Spanish American short-story writers; in technique, strength, and variety an accomplished master. His best stories afford us unforgettable portraits of the jungle province of Misiones, Argentina, where he spent a good part of his life. Poe and Kipling were his masters. His most famous work perhaps is *Cuentos de amor, de locura y de muerte.*

SUGGESTED READING: Selections from *Cuentos de amor, de locura y de muerte,* from *Anaconda,* and from texts recommended below.

TEXTS: Crow, 143–156. Holmes, *Span. Am.,* 480–482. Torres-Ríoseco, *Antología,* 94–99. Wilkins, 28–35.

EDITIONS: *Cuentos de amor, de locura y de muerte* (1917), 3d ed., Buenos Aires, Babel, 1925. *Anaconda* (1921), 2d ed., Buenos Aires, Babel, 1937. *El salvaje* (1920), 2d ed., Buenos Aires, Babel (192?). *El desierto,* Buenos Aires, Babel, 1924. *Cuentos,* 4 vols., Montevideo, La Bolsa de los Libros, 1937; ed. by O. Fernández Ríos.

TRANSLATIONS: Livingston, A. (trans.), *South American Jungle Tales* (*Cuentos de la selva*), New York, Duffield, 1922. Brenner, A. (trans.), "The Return of Anaconda" in Frank, 239–268.

CRITICAL REFERENCES: See texts above. •Crow, "La locura de Horacio Quiroga," *Revista iberoamericana,* I (1939), 33–45; see also his "La obra literaria de Horacio Quiroga," prologue to Quiroga, *Los perseguidos y otros cuentos,* Montevideo, Claudio García, [1940], 7–47. •Delgado, José M., and Brignole, Alberto J., *Vida y obra de Horacio Quiroga,* Montevideo, Claudio García, 1939. Englekirk, 340–368.

** 3. (URUGUAY) **Carlos Reyles** (1868–1938) was born into a well-to-do family and inherited a large fortune, and, except for considerable travel and his duties as lecturer in philosophy and literature at the University of Montevideo—a position created especially for him by the Chamber of Deputies—he devoted his entire life to his writing. His interest in letters, especially in the novel, was already compelling during his school years. He had an intimate knowledge of ranch life. Greatest of his country's novelists, he was a naturalist and a realist of varied style and theme. *El terruño,* which is probably his best novel, is a splendid study of rural life and of interesting psychological types, while *El embrujo de Sevilla,* written in the modernist manner, is considered one of the best works ever written about that Andalusian city.

SUGGESTED READING: *El terruño* or *El embrujo de Sevilla.*

TEXTS: Holmes, *Span. Am.,* 476–478. Torres-Ríoseco, *Antología,* 26–30.

EDITIONS: *El terruño,* Montevideo, Renacimiento, 1916. *El terruño,* Santiago, Ercilla, 1936. *El embrujo de Sevilla* (1922), Madrid, Sociedad General Española de Librería, 1927. *El embrujo de Sevilla,* Santiago, Ercilla, 1935. *El gaucho Florido,* Montevideo, Impresora Uruguaya, [1932]. *El gaucho Florido,* Buenos Aires, Espasa-Calpe, 1940 (Colección austral, 88).

TRANSLATION: LeClerq, J. (trans.), *Castanets* (*El embrujo de Sevilla*), London and New York, Longmans, 1929.

CRITICAL REFERENCES: See texts above. García Calderón, *Semblanzas,* 163–174. Rodó, "Prólogo" to *El terruño.* •Torres-Ríoseco, *Novelistas contemp.,* 311–351. Torres-Ríoseco, *Grandes novelistas,* 175–219. •Zum Felde, *Crítica,* 167–197.

\*  4. (ARGENTINA) **Enrique Rodríguez Larreta** (1875– ), minister plenipotentiary to France, 1910–1911, economically independent, has lived much abroad. He has always had a deep love for Spain and Hispanic tradition. He has written comparatively little. He won immediate and early fame for his *La gloria de don Ramiro,* a masterful reconstruction of Spanish life in the days of Philip II and considered one of the best historical novels in Spanish of all time. *Zogoibi,* his only other important work, represents his attempt to depict life on his native pampas, but the novel does not ring true. Larreta's style is polished and classic.

SUGGESTED READING: *La gloria de don Ramiro.*

EDITIONS: *La gloria de don Ramiro* (1908), Madrid, Espasa-Calpe, 1930. *La gloria de don Ramiro,* Buenos Aires, Espasa-Calpe, 1941 (Colección austral, 74). *Zogoibi,* Buenos Aires, Juan Roldán y Cía., 1926. *Zogoibi,* Buenos Aires, Espasa-Calpe, 1939 (Colección austral, 85).

TRANSLATION: Walton, L. B. (trans.), *The glory of Don Ramiro,* New York, Dutton, 1924.

CRITICAL REFERENCES: See texts above. Torres-Ríoseco, *Novela,* 219.

** 5. (ARGENTINA) **Manuel Gálvez** (1882– ) graduated from the Faculty of Law of Buenos Aires in 1904. Except for several trips to Europe and for his duties as supervisor of secondary education, his life has been devoted almost entirely to his writing. He is a realist of keen psychological insight. His style is simple and direct; his production is steady, varied, and uniformly good. The most popular novelist after Wast, Gálvez is also one of the most widely translated of Spanish American writers. *La maestra normal,* a convincing portrayal of the pettiness and monotony of provincial life, is his first— and possibly best—work. *Nacha Regules,* a novel of protest against the forces that impede the redemption of the heroine, continues to be a best-seller. Outstanding in American historical fiction is his trilogy on the Paraguayan war that appeared in 1928 and 1929. The recipient of several prizes, he was proposed by eminent writers and professors of both Americas as a candidate for the Nobel prize in literature.

SUGGESTED READING: *La maestra normal* or *La sombra del convento.*

EDITIONS: *La maestra normal* (1914), 4th ed., Buenos Aires, Agencia de Librería y Publicaciones, 1925. *La sombra del convento* (1917), Buenos Aires, Agencia General de Librería y Publicaciones, 1922. *Nacha Regules* (1919), Buenos Aires, Pax, 1920. *La tragedia de un hombre fuerte* (1922), Buenos Aires, Tor, 1938. *Escenas de la guerra del Paraguay:* I, *Los caminos de la muerte,* Buenos Aires, J. Roldán y Cía., 1928; II, *Humaitá,* Buenos Aires, J. Roldán y Cía., 1929; III, *Jornadas de agonía,* Buenos Aires, J. Roldán y Cía., 1929.

TRANSLATIONS: Ongley, L. (trans.), *Nacha Regules,* New York, Dutton, 1922. Wells, W. B. (trans.), *Holy Wednesday,* New York, Appleton-Century, 1934.

CRITICAL REFERENCES: See texts above. Coester, "Manuel Gálvez, Argentine Novelist," *Hispania,* V (1922), 325–335. Holmes, "Una trilogía de Manuel Gálvez: *Escenas de la guerra del Paraguay,*" *Revista hispánica moderna,* III (1937), 201–212. •Torres-Ríoseco, *Novelistas contemp.,* 251–270.

**6.** (ARGENTINA) **Hugo Wast** (pseudonym of Gustavo Martínez Zuviría) (1883– ), lawyer and one-time national deputy, has been director of the National Library since 1931. A "romancer" of bestsellers, not a few of them of questionable literary art, he is the most popular and most prolific of his country's novelists. His works have been translated into many languages.

SUGGESTED READING: *La casa de los cuervos* or *Desierto de piedra.*

TEXTS: Holmes, *Span. Am.,* 73–75. *La casa de los cuervos* (ed. Hespelt), New York, Macmillan, 1926. *Desierto de piedra* (ed. Sims), New York, Heath, 1930. *Pata de Zorra* (ed. Evans and Lind), Garden City, N. Y., Doubleday, 1937.

EDITIONS: *Flor de durazno* (1911), Buenos Aires, Agencia General de Librería y Publicaciones, [1927]. *La casa de los cuervos* (1916), Buenos Aires, Agencia General de Librería y Publicaciones, [1917]. *Desierto de piedra* (1925), Buenos Aires, Editores de Hugo Wast, 1938.

TRANSLATIONS: Matters, Leonard (trans.), *The House of the Ravens,* London, Williams and Norgate (1924). Hespelt, H. and M. (trans.), *Black Valley* (*Valle negro,* 1916), New York and London, Longmans, 1928. Hespelt, H. and M. (trans.), *Peach Blossom* (*Flor de durazno,* 1911), New York and London, Longmans, 1929. Imbert, L., and Le Clerq, J. (trans.), *Stone Desert,* New York and London, Longmans, 1929. Imbert, L., and Le Clerq, J.

(trans.), *The Strength of Lovers* (*Lucía Miranda*), London and New York, Longmans, 1930.

CRITICAL REFERENCES: See texts above. •Hespelt, E. Herman, "Hugo Wast—Argentine Novelist," *Hispania,* VII (1924), 360–367. •Sedgwick, Ruth, "Hugo Wast, Argentina's Most Popular Novelist," *Hispanic American Historical Review,* IX (1929), 116–126.

\*    7. (ARGENTINA) **Benito Lynch** (1885–    ), economically independent, has devoted all his time to his writing, but he is not a "littérateur." He has never lost contact with rural life. A master of gaucho jargon, he is the best and most popular of the living gaucho writers of his country. His style is simple and unadorned. His books afford excellent types and scenes of the pampas.

SUGGESTED READING: *El inglés de los güesos.*

TEXT: Torres-Ríoseco, *Antología,* 58–66.

EDITIONS: *Los caranchos de la Florida* (1916), 2d ed., Madrid, Espasa-Calpe, 1931. *Los caranchos de la Florida,* Buenos Aires, Espasa-Calpe, 1939 (Colección austral, 50). *El inglés de los güesos* (1924), Buenos Aires, La Facultad, 1937.

CRITICAL REFERENCES: See text above. •Torres-Ríoseco, *Novelistas contemp.,* 151–210. Torres-Ríoseco, *Grandes novelistas,* 111–171.

\*\*    8. (ARGENTINA) **Ricardo Güiraldes** (1886–1927), poet and short-story writer, traveled widely but never lost his deep love for "estancia" life, which he knew well. A vanguardist in style and a nationalist in temperament and themes, he has been generally acclaimed as the greatest of gaucho writers in prose for what is considered one of America's classics, *Don Segundo Sombra,* a perfect example of the application of modern technique to the treatment of a regional theme. His *Xaimaca,* a sentimental and impressionistic diary, is another fine example of postmodernist technique.

SUGGESTED READING: *Don Segundo Sombra.*

TEXTS: Holmes, *Span. Am.,* 75–78. Noé, 562–564 (poems). Onís, 964–967 (poems). Torres-Ríoseco, *Antología,* 73–78.

EDITIONS: *Xaimaca* (1923), Madrid, Espasa-Calpe, 1931. *Don Segundo Sombra* (1926), vol. 6 of *Obras,* Madrid, Espasa-Calpe, 1931–1933.

TRANSLATIONS: Onís, H. de (trans.), *Don Segundo Sombra* (*Shadows on the Pampas*), New York, Farrar and Rinehart, 1935. Brenner, A. (trans.), "Rosaura" in Frank, 181–235.

CRITICAL REFERENCES: See texts above. "Latin American Writers: Ricardo Güiraldes," *Panorama* [Pan-American Union], 16, Dec., 1940, 11–14. •Torres-Ríoseco, *Novelistas contemp.,* 123–149. Torres-Ríoseco, *Grandes novelistas,* 79–107.

\* **9.** (CHILE) **Eduardo Barrios** (1884– ), born in Valparaiso and educated in Santiago and Lima, wandered and worked in many countries of America before returning home to occupy several important posts during the twenties: among others, those of Director of National Libraries, Archives, and Museums and Minister of Public Education. He is one of America's outstanding cultivators of the psychological novel. His style is notable for its effortless simplicity. Artistry of a high order and skillful character portrayal make fascinating reading of *El hermano asno,* which, like his earlier novel cited below, is almost without action or plot. He has also written short stories and has won considerable fame as a dramatist.

SUGGESTED READING: *El hermano asno* or *El niño que enloqueció de amor.*

TEXTS: Holmes, *Span. Am.,* 171–173. Torres-Ríoseco, *Antología,* 53–57. Torres-Ríoseco and Kress, 23–30.

EDITIONS: *El niño que enloqueció de amor* (1915), Santiago, Nascimento, 1920. *Un perdido* (1917), Madrid, Espasa-Calpe, 1926. *El hermano asno* (1922), 2d ed., Santiago, Nascimento, 1937. *Páginas de un pobre diablo,* Santiago, Nascimento, 1923.

CRITICAL REFERENCES: See texts above. Díaz Arrieta, 78–80. Donoso, 153–180. Lillo, 418–422. •Torres-Ríoseco, *Novelistas contemp.*, 213–249.

10. (CHILE) **Mariano Latorre** (1886– ), professor and literary critic, has cultivated the short story with steadfast devotion for more than a quarter of a century. He has depicted almost every type and every phase of his country's rural life from the Andes (*Cuna de cóndores*) to the sea (*Chilenos del mar*). Characters and customs are generally subordinated to the natural setting. He is often characterized as the Chilean Pereda.

SUGGESTED READING: Selections in text recommended below.

TEXT: Leavitt, xiii–xv, 53–103 ("El piloto Oyarzo" and "El finado Valdés").

EDITIONS: *Cuentos del Maule*, Santiago, Zig-Zag, 1912. *Cuna de cóndores*, Santiago, Imprenta universitaria, 1918. *Chilenos del mar*, Santiago, Imprenta universitaria, 1929. *Hombres y zorros*, Santiago, Ercilla, 1937.

CRITICAL REFERENCES: See texts above. Amunátegui Solar, Domingo, *Las letras chilenas*, Santiago, Nascimento, 1934, 329–331. Díaz Arrieta, 81–83. Lillo, 441–442. •Silva Castro, 117–125.

11. (CHILE) **Pedro Prado** (1886– ), poet, architect, diplomat, and painter, has been the intellectual and aesthetic leader of his generation. In 1915 he founded the famous artistic circle "Los Diez," of which he was the guiding spirit and chronicler. One of America's finest stylists, he is at his best in his symbolic novel *Alsino*.

SUGGESTED READING: Selections in texts recommended below.

TEXTS: Holmes, *Span. Am.*, 155–157. Onís, 649–651. Torres-Ríoseco, *Antología*, 67–72.

EDITIONS: *Alsino* (1920), 2d ed., Santiago, Nascimento, 1928. *Un juez rural*, Santiago, Nascimento, 1924.

CRITICAL REFERENCES: See texts above. Díaz Arrieta, 92–99. Lillo, 439–440. •Torres-Ríoseco, *Novelistas contemp.,* 379–409.

12. (CHILE) **Joaquín Edwards Bello** (1888– ), journalist and editor of *La nación,* Santiago, since 1920, was educated in Chile and England. He has traveled widely. An aristocrat, he has championed the cause of the "roto," the man of the masses. A realist, he has written excellent sketches of the life of Chile's lower classes and of his countrymen abroad. His uneven, hurried, imperfect style is reminiscent of Baroja.

SUGGESTED READING: *El roto.*

TEXT: Torres-Ríoseco and Kress, 33–42.

EDITIONS: *El roto* (1920), 5th ed., Santiago, Nascimento, 1932. *El chileno en Madrid* (1928), 2d ed., Santiago, Nascimento, 1928.

CRITICAL REFERENCES: See text above. Díaz Arrieta, 87–92. Lillo, 459–460. Silva Castro, 137–151. •Torres-Ríoseco, *Novelistas contemp.,* 271–307.

13. (CHILE) **Manuel Rojas** (1896– ) was born in Buenos Aires of Chilean parents, but he has lived most of his life in Santiago. He has worked at various jobs from that of laborer on the trans-Andean railway to that of port sailor in Valparaiso. He finally took up journalism and since 1931 has been the manager of the University of Chile press. His vigorous stories, somber and ironic in tone, often reflect his own struggles and hardships.

SUGGESTED READING: Stories in texts cited below.

TEXTS: Crow, 157–170. Torres-Ríoseco and Kress, 3–12.

EDITIONS: *Hombres del sur,* Santiago, Nascimento, 1926; prologue by Raúl Silva Castro. *Lanchas en la bahía,* Santiago, Zig-Zag, 1932.

CRITICAL REFERENCES: See texts above. •Díaz Arrieta, 143–145. •Silva Castro, 163–179.

**14.** (PERU) **Enrique López Albújar** (1872– ) shares with Clorinda Matto de Turner (*Aves sin nido,* 1889) and Abraham Valdelomar (1888–1919) the distinction of having initiated the regional trend in Peruvian letters that produced in 1935 the prize-winning novel *La serpiente de oro*—the first great work to depict life in the Peruvian jungle—written by Ciro Alegría. Although a "limeño," López Albújar in his capacity as a public official came into direct and daily contact with the tragic existence of the Indians of the Andean highlands. Scarcely ever does a ray of light or hope flash over his dark pages. Regionalisms abound.

SUGGESTED READING: Selections from editions cited below.

EDITIONS: *Cuentos andinos* (1920), Lima, Imprenta Lux, 1924. *Nuevos cuentos andinos,* Santiago, Ercilla, 1937.

CRITICAL REFERENCE: Rubio, David, *"Nuevos cuentos andinos,"* *Revista iberoamericana,* II (1940), 511–514.

**15.** (BOLIVIA) **Alcides Arguedas** (1879– ) was educated in La Paz and pursued special studies in the social sciences in Paris. He has represented his country in the diplomatic service in London, Paris, and Colombia. A journalist, sociologist, and historian, he is Bolivia's most prominent writer of our time. In his first novel, *Wuatu-Wuaru* (1904), he stands out as a precursor of the new "indianista" literature in which the Indian is presented as a pressing social problem. His best work, *Raza de bronce,* affords a dark, depressing picture of Bolivia's native masses. *Pueblo enfermo* is one of the best literary-sociological studies yet written on the American Indian problem.

SUGGESTED READING: Selections in texts cited below.

TEXTS: Holmes, *Span. Am.,* 109–112. Torres-Ríoseco, *Antología,* 39–42.

EDITIONS: *Pueblo enfermo* (1909), Santiago, Ercilla, 1937. *Vida criolla,* Paris, 1912. *Raza de bronce,* La Paz, González y Medina, 1919.

CRITICAL REFERENCES: See texts above. •Guzmán, 106–113. Torres-Ríoseco, *Novela,* 225–226.

16. (ECUADOR) **Jorge Icaza** (1902– ) is probably one of the most representative and best of the young Ecuadorian writers who in the past decade have denounced the shameless exploitation of their country's Indian masses. In 1935 he was awarded the national prize for *En las calles.* However, his artistry is often marred by heavy overtones of stark, brutal realism; this is particularly true of *Cholos,* his latest important work.

SUGGESTED READING: *En las calles.*

EDITIONS: *Huasipungo* (1934), 5th ed., Quito, Tipo-Lito "Romero," 1937. *En las calles,* Quito, Imprenta Nacional, 1935. *Cholos,* Quito, Sindicato de Escritores y Artistas, 1938.

TRANSLATION: *Huasipungo* in *International Literature* (Moscow), Feb., 1936.

CRITICAL REFERENCES: •Franklin, A. B., *"Cholos," The Quarterly Journal of Inter-American Relations,* I (1939), 131–133; see also his "Ecuador's Novelists at Work," *Inter-American Quarterly,* II (1940), 37–38. •Suárez Calimano, E., "Dos novelas de Jorge Icaza," *Nosotros,* I [2nd series] (1936), 315–319. Torres-Ríoseco, *Novela,* 234–235; see also his "Nuevas tendencias en la novela," *Revista iberoamericana,* I (1939), 91–94.

** 17. (COLOMBIA) **José Eustasio Rivera** (1889–1928), lawyer and poet [see Section E, V, 1, d, (1)], was born in the tropical city of Neiva in southern Colombia and died in New York, where he was enjoying a recent literary triumph. Government commissions afforded him the opportunity to know and study at first hand the region and types he later described in his single prose work, which has been acclaimed one of the great American novels and probably the best yet written in Spanish on the American tropics. Poetic in style, romantic in spirit, and sociological in content, *La vorágine* is an impassioned denunciation of the tragedy that befell the Colombian rubber gatherers in the upper Amazon jungle over a generation ago.

SUGGESTED READING: *La vorágine.*

TEXTS: Holmes, *Span. Am.,* 247–249. Torres-Ríoseco, *Antología,* 79–81.

EDITIONS: *La vorágine* (1924), Buenos Aires, Biblioteca Universal, 1931. *La vorágine,* Buenos Aires, Espasa-Calpe, 1941 (Colección austral, 35).

TRANSLATION: James, E. K. (trans.), *The Vortex,* New York, Putnam, 1935.

CRITICAL REFERENCES: •Neale-Silva, Eduardo, "The Factual Bases of *La vorágine,*" *PMLA,* LIV (1939), 316–331. •Torres-Ríoseco, *Novelistas contemp.,* 45–90. Torres-Ríoseco, *Grandes novelistas,* 223–272.

** **18.** (VENEZUELA) **Rómulo Gallegos** (1884– ), educator and professor, became a voluntary political exile in 1931, living in Spain from that year until after the death of Gómez in 1935. Upon his return he entered politics to become one of the three presidential candidates in the 1941 elections. He began his literary career in the field of the short story and the theater, not turning to the novel until the early twenties. As a novelist he is a master of plot technique. His easy, natural style is notable for its poetic quality. A realist of marked romantic leanings, he excels in depicting the way of life of the "llanero," the Venezuelan man of the plains. His *Doña Bárbara* is another American "classic," the Venezuelan counterpart in fiction of Sarmiento's account of his country's struggle between "barbarie" and "civilización." *Cantaclaro* is a beautiful tribute to the native bards and ballads for which his country is famous.

SUGGESTED READING: *Doña Bárbara* or *Cantaclaro* or *Canaima.*

TEXTS: *Doña Bárbara* (ed. Dunham), New York, Crofts, 1942. Torres-Ríoseco, *Antología,* 50–52.

EDITIONS: *Doña Bárbara* (1929), 7th ed., Barcelona, Araluce, n.d. *Cantaclaro* (1931), 3d ed., Barcelona, Araluce, 1934. *Canaima* (1935), 4th ed., Barcelona, Araluce, 1936.

TRANSLATION: Malloy, R. (trans.), *Doña Bárbara,* New York, Cape and Smith, 1931.

CRITICAL REFERENCES: See texts above. González, Manuel P., "A propósito de *Doña Bárbara,*" *Bulletin of Spanish Studies,* VII (1930), 162–167. Picón-Salas, 217–220. •Ratcliff, 235–263. •Torres-Ríoseco, *Novelistas contemp.,* 91–122. Torres-Ríoseco, *Grandes novelistas,* 43–76.

19. (VENEZUELA) **Teresa de la Parra** (1895–1936) received most of her education in Paris, where she spent much of her short life. She is probably the most original and most charming of American women prose writers. In an inimitable personal style, she has penned delightful sketches of Venezuelan rural life. *Las memorias de Mamá Blanca* (1929), a book of childhood reminiscences, ranks high in American autobiographical fiction.

SUGGESTED READING: *Las memorias de Mamá Blanca* in text edition cited below.

TEXTS: *Las memorias de Mamá Blanca* (ed. García-Prada and Wilson), New York, Macmillan, 1932. Holmes, *Span. Am.,* 537–541.

EDITIONS: *Ifigenia* (1924), 2d ed., Santiago, Zig-Zag, [1937]. *Las memorias de Mamá Blanca,* Paris, Le Livre Libre, 1929.

CRITICAL REFERENCES: See texts above. •Ratcliff, 214–232.

20. (CUBA) **Carlos Loveira** (1882–1928) grew up as an orphan on the streets of New York. At sixteen he joined a filibustering expedition to his native land. That was the beginning of a turbulent career in which he lived and fought for the underprivileged in almost

every country of the Caribbean world. A propagandist and social critic, he is the most vigorous novelist his country has yet produced. His themes are largely autobiographical, his style journalistic.

SUGGESTED READING: *Juan Criollo*.

TEXT: Holmes, *Span. Am.*, 293–296.

EDITIONS: *Los ciegos,* Habana, El Siglo XX, 1922. *Juan Criollo,* Habana, Cultural, 1927.

CRITICAL REFERENCES: See text above. Coester, *Lit. Hist.,* 487–489. •González, M. P., "Carlos Loveira," *Revista de estudios hispánicos,* II (1929), 177–193.

* **21.** (GUATEMALA) **Rafael Arévalo Martínez** (1884–    ), poet [see Section E, V, 1, c, (1)] and novelist, has been director of the National Library since 1926. The creator of an original and interesting type of short story known as the psychozoological tale, he is one of the leading representatives of universal imaginative fiction in America today. His outstanding work is the novelette *El hombre que parecía un caballo* (1915).

SUGGESTED READING: *El hombre que parecía un caballo*.

TEXT: Torres-Ríoseco, *Antología,* 107–113.

EDITIONS: *El hombre que parecía un caballo y Las rosas de Engaddi,* Guatemala, Sánchez y de Guise, 1927. *El Señor Monitot,* Guatemala, Sánchez y de Guise, 1922. *El mundo de los Maharachías,* Guatemala, Muñoz Plaza y Cía., 1938. *Viaje a Ipanda,* Guatemala, Centro Editorial, 1939.

TRANSLATIONS: Clark, Victor S. (trans.), "Our Lady of the Afflicted" ("Nuestra Señora de los locos") and "The Panther Man" ("Las fieras del trópico"), *The Living Age,* vol. 321 (1924), 800–806, 1005–1011, 1046–1052.

CRITICAL REFERENCES: See text above. Englekirk, 369–385. •Onís, "Resurrección de Arévalo Martínez," *Revista de estudios hispánicos,* I (1928), 290–295. •Torres-Ríoseco, *Novelistas contemp.,* 411–422.

** 22. (MEXICO) **Mariano Azuela** (1873– ) was born in Lagos de Moreno, Jalisco. He received most of his education in Guadalajara, where he studied medicine, returning to practice in his native city. He wrote his first pieces when still a medical student. Ever since those early years he has pursued his double role of doctor and novelist. For several months in 1915 he served as army doctor in one of Villa's bands. In 1916 he moved to Mexico City. He is the only true novelist the Revolution has produced. He has treated and interpreted every phase of the movement from the last days of Díaz to the close of Cárdenas' term as president. *Los de abajo* (1915), a "modern classic," is a series of deeply etched sketches of the "blood-and-horror" years of the Revolution. It has been translated into almost every major living language.

SUGGESTED READING: *Los de abajo.*

TEXTS: *Los de abajo* (ed. Englekirk and Kiddle), New York, Crofts, 1939. Torres-Ríoseco, *Antología,* 31–33.

EDITIONS: *Mala yerba* (1909), Mexico, Botas, 1937. *Los de abajo* (1915), Mexico, Robredo, 1938. *Los caciques* and *Las moscas* (1917), Mexico, La Razón, 1931. *La luciérnaga,* Madrid, Espasa-Calpe, 1932.

TRANSLATIONS: Munguía, Enrique (trans.), *The Underdogs,* New York, Brentano's, 1929. Brenner, Anita (trans.), *Marcela* (*Mala yerba*), New York, Farrar and Rinehart, 1932.

CRITICAL REFERENCES: See texts above. •Torres-Ríoseco, *Novelistas contemp.,* 11–44. Torres-Ríoseco, *Grandes novelistas,* 3–40.

23. (MEXICO) **Martín Luis Guzmán** (1887– ) was born in Chihuahua and studied law in the University of Mexico. He was a journalist with the forces of the Revolution in the north. From 1914 to 1934 he spent most of his years as an exile in New York and in Madrid.

After Azuela, he was the earliest outstanding novelist to record his experiences and impressions of the war years (*El águila y la serpiente*) and of the political intrigue and corruption of the twenties (*La sombra del caudillo*).

SUGGESTED READING: *El águila y la serpiente.*

EDITIONS: *El águila y la serpiente* (1928), 3d ed., Madrid, Espasa-Calpe, 1932. *La sombra del caudillo* (1929), 3d ed., Mexico, Botas, 1938..

TRANSLATION: Onís, H. de (trans.), *The Eagle and the Serpent,* New York, Knopf, 1930.

CRITICAL REFERENCES: González Peña, 295. •Houck, Helen P., "Las obras novelescas de Martín Luis Guzmán," *Revista ibero-americana,* III (1941), 139–158.

* **24.** (MEXICO) **Gregorio López y Fuentes** (1895– ) was born in the State of Veracruz, where he taught for some time as schoolmaster among the Indians. Later he came to the capital to take up journalism. He began his literary career as a poet. His first novel (*Campamento*) did not appear until 1931. He is the youngest and most promising of the novelists of the Revolution. He writes in a vigorous, personal style. He is especially interested in the revolutionary program as it pertains to the land and to the Indian. In 1935 he was awarded the first national prize in literature for *El indio.*

SUGGESTED READING: *El indio.*

TEXT: *El indio* (ed. Hespelt), New York, Norton, 1940.

EDITIONS: *Tierra,* Mexico, Editorial México, 1933. *¡Mi General!,* Mexico, Botas, 1934. *El indio* (1935), 2d ed., Mexico, Botas, 1937.

TRANSLATION: Brenner, Anita (trans.), *El indio,* Indianapolis, Bobbs-Merrill, 1937.

CRITICAL REFERENCES: See text above. González Peña, 296. •Moore, Ernest R., "Gregorio López y Fuentes," *Mexican Life,* XVI (1940), 23 ff.

**25.** (MEXICO) **José Rubén Romero** (1890– ) was born in the province of Michoacán, where he spent most of his youth. In 1911 he took part in the Madero revolt. In 1917 he entered politics; his rise was rapid; since 1937 he has been ambassador to Brazil and to Cuba. He wrote his first poem in 1902; his first novel did not appear until 1933. A regionalist of racy, colorful style, he has etched unforgettable types and scenes of Michoacán. *La vida inútil de Pito Pérez* places him among America's most promising cultivators of the picaresque genre.

SUGGESTED READING: *La vida inútil de Pito Pérez.*

EDITIONS: *Desbandada,* Mexico, 1934. *El pueblo inocente* (1934), 2d ed., Mexico, Impr. Mundial, 1934. *La vida inútil de Pito Pérez,* Mexico, México Nuevo, 1938.

CRITICAL REFERENCES: González Peña, 296–297. La Farga, Gastón, *La evolución literaria de Rubén Romero,* Mexico, n. p., 1939. ●Moore, Ernest R., *Novelistas de la Revolución Mexicana: J. Rubén Romero,* Habana, Colección "el ciervo herido," 1940.

## V. Poetry.

The poets are somewhat confused. On one point only are they in agreement: they concur in that the more significant innovations of their predecessors must be purified and perfected and definitely incorporated into the poetry of the future. But in all else so diverse are the paths they follow that it is impossible to attempt any clear-cut definition of their aesthetics as a group. Two tendencies, however, may be said to characterize their departure from the modernist school proper: one, to return to simplicity and directness of expression and to traditional and popular themes and forms; the other, to carry to its ultimate possibilities that phase of the modernist movement (obscure imagery, free verse) that tended to divorce poetry from all that man has associated with it in the past. The first tendency is particularly characteristic of the period between 1910 and 1918, and it is to this movement that critics usually refer as post-modernism. The movement, however, continues to our day as one of the more pronounced manifestations of the revolt against the earlier phases of modernism. In an effort to classify still further the many poets deserving of mention in this postmodernist period, we have grouped them as follows: (a) the feminine group; (b) those who strive for simplicity of expression and form; (c) those who through irony and humor ridicule the excesses of their predecessors; and (d) those who capture in their poetry either the natural setting or the social scene. The second tendency first appears in the closing years of the First World War and continues, somewhat less nihilistic and with modifications, down to the present time. Exponents of this type of poetry are generally classified as "ultraístas."

REFERENCES: Commentary, criticism, and bibliography, by Craig, Holmes, Onís, and Torres-Ríoseco, in their respective anthologies. Coester, *Lit. Hist.*, 481–486. Sánchez, *Hist. de la lit. am.*, 556–595. See Blackwell and Craig for selections and English versions of poems by many poets of this period.

1. Postmodernists.

a. The feminine group.

(1). (URUGUAY) **Delmira Agustini** (1890–1914) was born into a wealthy family and received the type of cultural education befitting a young lady of Montevideo society. An unhappy marriage soon ended in separation; a short time afterward she was killed by her estranged husband. When but a child she experienced a great passion for music and for poetry. Her earliest volume of verse, *El libro blanco,* was published in Montevideo in 1907. Modernist tendencies carry over in most of her work, of which the predominant theme is impassioned love. She is considered by some critics as the greatest of Spanish American women poets.

SUGGESTED READING: Selections in texts recommended below.

TEXTS: Holmes, *Span. Am.,* 461–462. Onís, 907–920. Solar Correa, 217–218. Torres-Ríoseco, *Antología,* 281–283.

EDITIONS: *Obras completas,* Montevideo, M. García, 1924. *Las mejores poesías,* Barcelona, Cervantes, n.d. *Poesías,* Montevideo, Claudio García, 1939; introduced by Ovidio Fernández Ríos.

CRITICAL REFERENCES: See texts above. •Miranda, 154–195.

**    (2). (CHILE) Gabriela Mistral** (pseudonym of Lucila Godoy Azcayaga) (1889– ) was born in the provinces. For almost a decade she served as teacher and director of schools in many parts of the country. In 1922 she came to Santiago, already acclaimed for the poetry she had written during her years of teaching and soon to be rewarded for her educational work by being appointed the nation's delegate to several international gatherings. She has lectured and traveled widely in America and Europe. Because of an early tragic love affair she has never married. Her verse is strongly mystic, often uneven. Poetic themes are children and unsatisfied maternal longing. Her first and best collection, entitled *Desolación,* was published in New York in 1922.

SUGGESTED READING: Selections in texts recommended below.

TEXTS: Blackwell, 236–279. Craig, 194–205. Holmes, *Span. Am.,* 157–161. Onís, 920–932. Solar Correa, 229–237. Torres-Ríoseco, *Antología,* 284–286. Weisinger, 230–239.

EDITIONS: *Desolación,* New York, Instituto de las Españas, 1922. *Desolación,* 3d ed., Santiago, Nascimento, [1926]. *Las mejores poesías,* 2d ed., Barcelona, Cervantes, [1936].

TRANSLATIONS: Blackwell, 236–279. Craig, 194–205. Walsh, *Hisp. Anth.,* 735–736.

CRITICAL REFERENCES: See texts above. •Díaz Arrieta, 68–75. Donoso, 37–65. Miranda, 24–64. •Silva Castro, 151–163.

(3). (ARGENTINA) **Alfonsina Storni** (1892–1938) was born in Switzerland but reared in the Argentine provinces of San Juan and Santa Fe. When still very young she came to Buenos Aires, where first in business and later in teaching she worked hard to make a living for herself and her family. Journalism and poetry rounded out the activities of her hurried life, which she herself brought to an untimely end. Her first volume, *La inquietud del rosal,* appeared in 1916. Themes that recur again and again are: love and sexual desire and womanly instincts and feelings as both an individual and a social problem. Her verse is markedly intellectual, yet rich in emotional range.

SUGGESTED READING: Selections in texts recommended below.

TEXTS: Blackwell, 387–391. Craig, 220–225. Holmes, *Span. Am.,* 53. Noé, 424–439. Onís, 932–941. Solar Correa, 238–240. Torres-Ríoseco, *Antología,* 287–290.

EDITIONS: *Las mejores poesías,* Barcelona, Cervantes, [1923]. *Antología poética* (1915–1938), Buenos Aires, Espasa-Calpe, 1938.

TRANSLATIONS: Blackwell, 387–391. Craig, 220–225.

CRITICAL REFERENCES: See texts above. Mañach, Jorge, "La liberación de Alfonsina Storni," *Revista iberoamericana,* I (1939), 73–76. •Peyro de Martínez Ferrer, Gra-

ciela, "La obra lírica de Alfonsina Storni," *Nosotros,* VIII
(1938), 252–265.

**(4).** (Uruguay) **Juana de Ibarbourou** (1895– ) was born in the
provincial city of Melo, where she lived until her early and
happy marriage at the age of eighteen, when she moved to
Montevideo. Her simple, uneventful life has been that of
a contented and loving wife and mother. The most beloved of America's women poets, she was christened in
1929 with the deserved name "Juana de América." *Las
lenguas de diamante,* her first volume, appeared in 1918.
Her verse is simple, sensuous, and intensely subjective;
poetic themes are nature and exaltation of a satisfied love.

Suggested Reading: Selections in texts recommended below.

Texts: Blackwell, 448–449. Holmes, *Span. Am.,* 462–
463. Onís, 941–951. Solar Correa, 241–244. Torres-Ríoseco, *Antología,* 291–294.

Editions: *Las mejores poesías,* edición homenaje, Barcelona, Cervantes, 1930. *Sus mejores poemas,* Madrid, Editorial-América, 1930; prologue by Rufino Blanco-Fombona.
*Sus mejores poemas,* Santiago, Nascimento, 1930; selección
y prólogo de H. Díaz Casanueva.

Translation: Blackwell, 448–449.

Critical References: See texts and editions above. •Mi-
randa, 195–247.

**b.** Poets advocating simplicity of expression and form.

**(1).** (Chile) **Manuel Magallanes Moure** (1878–1924), painter
and critic of art and letters, was a member of the famous
circle of "Los Diez." He has been rightfully called the
precursor of contemporary Chilean poetry. Modernist
influences are apparent in most of his work, but were
held in check by the simplicity, sincerity, and dignity that

characterized both his art and his life. *Facetas,* his first work, was published in 1902.

SUGGESTED READING: Selections in texts recommended below.

TEXTS: Blackwell, 298–301. Holmes, *Span. Am.,* 150–152. Onís, 637–645. Solar Correa, 205–208.

EDITIONS: *Florilegio,* San José de Costa Rica, 1921; selected by author, prologue by Pedro Prado. *Sus mejores poemas,* Santiago, Nascimento, 1926; edited by Pedro Prado.

TRANSLATIONS: Blackwell, 298–301. Walsh, *Hisp. Anth.,* 689–691.

CRITICAL REFERENCES: See texts above. Díaz Arrieta, 19–21. •Silva Castro, 65–77.

**

(2). (ARGENTINA) **Enrique Banchs** (1888– ) is the first of his country's great poets after Lugones. His verse is simple and unpretentious, rich in popular forms and themes. His first volume, *Las barcas,* appeared in 1907. His literary activity was intense until 1911. Since then, in spite of the success of those early volumes, he has published only four other works.

SUGGESTED READING: Selections in texts recommended below.

TEXTS: Craig, 174–181. Holmes, *Span. Am.,* 50–51. Noé, 181–197. Onís, 703–714. Torres-Ríoseco, *Antología,* 274–275.

EDITIONS: *El cascabel del halcón,* Buenos Aires, La Editorial Argentina, 1909. *Poemas selectos,* Mexico, A. Loera Chávez, 1921; edition and prologue by F. Monterde.

TRANSLATIONS: Craig, 174–181.

CRITICAL REFERENCES: See texts above.

* (3). (Argentina) **Rafael Alberto Arrieta** (1889– ) was educated at the universities of La Plata and Buenos Aires,
where he later taught as professor of European literature
from 1912 to 1928. He has held several other academic
posts since, but his one great devotion has been letters.
He has taken an active interest in literary journalism and
has written significant critical studies of great European
writers. His verse is marked by simplicity, serenity, and
predilection for humble, daily themes and traditional
forms. *Alma y momento,* his first work, appeared in
Buenos Aires in 1918.

SUGGESTED READING: Selections in texts recommended below.

TEXTS: Holmes, *Span. Am.,* 49–50. Noé, 169–180. Onís,
659–665. Torres-Ríoseco, *Antología,* 278.

EDITION: *Sus mejores poemas,* Buenos Aires, Agencia
General de Librería y Publicaciones, 1923.

CRITICAL REFERENCES: See texts above.

** (4). (Mexico) **Ramón López Velarde** (1888–1921), journalist
and professor, was born in the State of Zacatecas. Although markedly a regionalist in themes and emotions,
he soon distinguished himself in artistic expression as the
most daring of the postmodernist poets of his country. His
early death cut short an artistic production of unusual
promise. Two of his works were published posthumously:
*El minutero,* a volume of prose, and *El son del corazón.*
*La sangre devota,* his first published work, appeared in
1916.

SUGGESTED READING: Selections in texts recommended below.

TEXTS: Castro Leal, 275–284. Onís, 967–974. Torres-
Ríoseco, *Antología,* 276–277.

EDITIONS: *Poemas escogidos,* Mexico, Cultura, 1935; with a critical study by Xavier Villaurrutia. *Selección de poesías,* Mexico, Ed. Orientaciones, 1938.

TRANSLATIONS: Underwood, 66–69.

CRITICAL REFERENCES: See texts and editions above.

**c.** Poets of satire and irony.

**\*\***     **(1).** (GUATEMALA) **Rafael Arévalo Martínez** (1884– ) (see Section E, IV, 21), is a disciple of the later Darío of *Cantos de vida y esperanza,* of whom he was an ardent admirer. He is a master of poetic technique. Subjective and religious in theme, sentimental and ironic in spirit, his poetry is reminiscent of the best of classic Spanish expression. His first volume of verse, *Maya,* was published in Guatemala in 1911.

SUGGESTED READING: Selections in texts recommended below.

TEXTS: Blackwell, 474–477. Holmes, 131. \*Onís, 857–864.

EDITIONS: *Los atormentados,* Guatemala, Unión Tipográfica, 1914. *El hombre que parecía un caballo y Las rosas de Engaddi,* Guatemala, Sánchez y de Guise, 1927. *Llama,* Mexico, Imprenta Mundial, 1934.

TRANSLATIONS: Blackwell, 474–477. Walsh, *Hisp. Anth.,* 729–734.

CRITICAL REFERENCES: See texts above. See Section E, IV, 21.

**\***     **(2).** (COLOMBIA) **Luis Carlos López** (1880– ) was born in Cartagena, where he has spent the whole of an apparently uneventful life. Regional in theme, satiric and ironic in spirit, he is typical of the postmodernist who mocks the excesses of his school and of his age. Long denied the recognition he justly deserves, he has written inimitable poetic sketches of scenes and types of his "ciudad nativa." *De mi villorio,* his first volume, appeared in Madrid in 1908.

SUGGESTED READING: Selections in texts recommended below.

TEXTS: García-Prada, II, 181–197. Holmes, *Span. Am.,* 241. Onís, 851–857.

EDITIONS: *De mi villorio,* Madrid, Imprenta de la Revista de Archivos, 1908; prologue by Manuel Cervera. *Posturas difíciles,* Bogotá, 1909. *Por el atajo,* Cartagena, 1928; prologue by Sanín Cano.

TRANSLATIONS: Walsh, *Hisp. Anth.,* 711–714.

CRITICAL REFERENCES: See texts above. García Godoy, *La lit. amer.,* 169–174. •Llorente Arroyo, A., "Luis Carlos López," *Hispania,* VII (1924), 377–386.

**d.** Poets of American themes.

(1). (COLOMBIA) **José Eustasio Rivera** (1889–1929) (see Section E, IV, 17) is the poet of the tropics and the jungle, which he describes with the same realistic touches that characterize his novel. His only collection, *Tierra de promisión,* is one of the fine volumes of American sonnets.

SUGGESTED READING: Selections in texts recommended below.

TEXTS: García-Prada, II, 289–301. Onís, 837–841.

EDITIONS: *Tierra de promisión* (1921), 2d ed., Santiago, Ercilla, 1938.

CRITICAL REFERENCES: See texts above. See Section E, IV, 17.

(2). (CUBA) **Nicolás Guillén** (1904– ) and Luis Palés Matos, the Puerto Rican, are the leading "nativist" poets of the

Caribbean. Their work is closely akin to that of our own school of Negro poets and poets of Negro themes and rhythms. A mulatto, Guillén has made of *Sóngoro cosongo* one of the earliest and best expressions of spiritual fusion of white and black in America. All of his verse is intensely racial in character and folkloric in theme.

SUGGESTED READING: Selections in texts recommended below.

TEXTS: Guirao, Ramón, *Orbita de la poesía afrocubana, 1928-37 (Antología)*, Habana, Ucar, García y Cía., 1938, 84-104. Onís, 1025-1026.

EDITIONS: *Motivos de son,* Habana, 1930. *Sóngoro cosongo,* Habana, 1931.

CRITICAL REFERENCES: See texts above. •Marinello, 79-93.

2. Ultraístas.

a. (CHILE) **Vicente Huidobro** (1893- ) announced his conception of the new poetry in Buenos Aires in 1916; in 1918 he appeared in Spain as the founder of "creacionismo." His absolute and continued denial of the entire poetic past marks him as the precursor and greatest exponent of one of the many aesthetic movements of the postwar period that failed to survive or to blossom out into a rich enduring poetic contribution. His influence has been limited to the ephemeral movements he created. His first collection, *Ecos del alma,* was published in Santiago in 1910. Much of his later work has been written in French.

SUGGESTED READING: Selections in texts recommended below.

TEXTS: Craig, 236-243. Holmes, *Span. Am.,* 162. Onís, 1127-1133.

EDITIONS: *Poemas árticos,* Madrid, Imprenta Pueyo, 1918. *Vientos contrarios,* Santiago, Nascimento, 1926.

TRANSLATIONS: Craig, 236–243.

CRITICAL REFERENCES: See texts above. Díaz Arrieta, 111–113. •Holmes, Henry A., *Vicente Huidobro and Creationism,* New York, Institute of French Studies, 1933; also his "The Creationism of Vicente Huidobro," *The Spanish Review,* I (1934), 9–16.

* **b.** (ARGENTINA) **Jorge Luis Borges** (1899– ) was born in Buenos Aires and educated in Switzerland. He was one of the group of "ultraístas" in Spain in 1918. In 1921 he returned to Buenos Aires to initiate the movement there. The novel imagery of his poetry is rendered more intelligible than that of Huidobro because of strong classic ties and his love of the national past. He published his first volume of verse, *Fervor de Buenos Aires,* in 1923.

SUGGESTED READING: Selections in texts recommended below.

TEXTS: Craig, 244–247. Holmes, *Span. Am.,* 54–55. Noé, 470–476. Onís, 1149–1154.

EDITIONS: *Fervor de Buenos Aires,* Buenos Aires, 1923. *Luna de enfrente,* Buenos Aires, Proa, 1925.

TRANSLATIONS: Craig, 244–247.

CRITICAL REFERENCES: See texts above.

* **c.** (MEXICO) **Jaime Torres Bodet** (1902– ) graduated from the University of Mexico, where he taught French literature from 1924 to 1928. He has been in the diplomatic service—in Spain and Holland and at present in France—since 1929. He has published more than seventeen volumes of verse and prose since his first collection of poems, *Fervor,* was published in Mexico in 1918. His verse progresses from lyric simplicity to the most recent innovations of French schools.

SUGGESTED READING: Selections in texts recommended below.

TEXTS: Blackwell, 165–167. Holmes, *Span. Am.,* 378. Onís, 995–1002.

EDITIONS: *Poemas,* Mexico, Herrero, 1924. *Biombo,* Mexico, Herrero, 1925. *Destierro,* Madrid, Espasa-Calpe, 1930.

TRANSLATIONS: Underwood, 172–177.

CRITICAL REFERENCES: See texts above. Llanos, A., "La poesía de Torres Bodet," *Abside,* [Mexico], II (1938), 28–36.

** **d.** (CHILE) **Pablo Neruda** (pseudonym of Neftalí Reyes) (1904– ) has been in the consular service since 1927, in the Far East, in Buenos Aires, and presently in Mexico. He has been acclaimed as one of the most gifted of America's younger poets. A great admirer of García Lorca, he has written a fine essay on the Spanish poet which has done much toward making his poetry known throughout Spanish America. His art is the product of a romantic and dramatic outlook on life. Extreme subjectivity is the salient feature of his verse. *La canción de la fiesta,* Santiago, 1921, is his first published work.

SUGGESTED READING: Selections in texts recommended below.

TEXTS: Craig, 226–235. Holmes, *Span. Am.,* 163–164. Onís, 1154–1159.

EDITIONS: *Crepusculario* (1919), 2nd ed., Santiago, Nascimento, 1926. *Veinte poemas de amor y una canción desesperada* (1924), 5th ed., Santiago, Ercilla, 1938. *Residencia en la tierra* (*1925–1931*) (1933), 3d ed., Santiago, Ercilla, 1938. *España en el corazón,* Santiago, Ercilla, 1937.

TRANSLATIONS: Craig, 226–235.

CRITICAL REFERENCES: See texts above. •Alonso, Amado, "Algunos símbolos insistentes en la poesía de Pablo Neruda," *Revista hispánica moderna,* V (1939), 191–220. •Díaz Arrieta, 116–121. Silva Castro, 199–217.

# A Bibliographical Introduction to Brazilian Literature for Those Reading Only English and Spanish

## LITERARY HISTORY AND CRITICISM

Arruda Botelho, Antonio de, "Panorama de la moderna literatura brasileña," *América,* Havana, IX (1941), 52–57.

Ayala Duarte, Crispín, "Sobre la literatura del Brasil," *Boletín de la Academia Venezolana,* Año IV (1937), 81–119.

Besouchet, Lidia, and Freitas, Newton, *Diez escritores de Brasil,* Buenos Aires, Gleizer, 1939.

Carvalho, Ronald de, "The Brazilian Novel," *Inter-America,* English: VI (1922), 214–221.

Ford, J. D. M., and others, *A Tentative Bibliography of Brazilian Belles-Lettres,* Cambridge, Harvard Univ. Press, 1931.

García Mérou, Martín, *El Brasil intelectual: impresiones y notas literarias,* Buenos Aires, Lajouane, 1900.

Goldberg, Isaac, *Brazilian Literature,* New York, Knopf, 1922.

Goldberg, Isaac, *The Spirit of Brazilian Literature,* Girard, Kansas, Haldeman-Julius, [1924] (Little Blue Book 646).

Hanke, Lewis (ed.), *Handbook of Latin American Studies,* Cambridge, Harvard Univ. Press, 1935– , annually; section on Brazil by Samuel Putnam.

Lima, Herman, "The Short Story," *Inter-America,* English: VI (1922), 303–311.

Ramsey, M. M., "Latin-American Literature," in Warner (ed.), *A Library of the World's Best Literature Ancient and Modern,* New York, The International Society, 1897, Vol. XXII, 8903–8928, *passim.*

Sánchez Sáez, Braulio, *Vieja y nueva literatura del Brasil,* Santiago de Chile, Ercilla, 1935.

## BRAZILIAN POETRY IN ENGLISH AND SPANISH TRANSLATIONS

### ANTHOLOGIES

Bustamente y Ballivián, Enrique, *Poetas brasileros (traducción anotada)*: *Románticos, parnasianos, symbolistas, poetas nuevos,* Rio de Janeiro, Emp. Ind. Ed. "O Norte," 1922.

Casas, Alvaro de las (trans.), *Sonetos brasileños traducidos al español,* prólogo del Dr. Claudio de Souza, presidente de la Academia, Rio de Janeiro, [Gráfica Sauer], 1938.

Poor, Agnes Blake, *Pan-American Poems,* Boston, The Gorham Press, 1918.

Teixeira, Mucio, *Brasileñas y lusitanas (poesías),* Caracas, 1889.

Walsh, Thomas, *Hispanic Anthology,* New York and London, Putnam, 1920.

### WORKS BY OR ABOUT INDIVIDUAL POETS

ANTONIO GONÇALVES DIAZ (1823–1864)
*Poesías americanas del poeta brasileño Antonio Gonçalves Diaz tra-ducidas en verso castellano* por Julio Vicuña Cifuentes, Santiago de Chile, Imp. Cervantes, 1903.

ANTONIO DE CASTRO ALVES (1847–1871)
*El navío negrero y otros poemas de Castro Alves,* Madrid, Pueyo, 1930; translations by Francisco Villaespesa.

JOÃO DA CRUZ Y SOUZA (1863–1898)
Guido, Angel, *El poeta negro Cruz e Souza,* Buenos Aires, Edgard, n.d.

OLAVO BRAZ MARTINS DOS GUIMARÃES BILAC (1865–1919)
*Los viajes,* Havana, Alfa, 1940; translations by Rafael Esténger.
*Sonetos,* Buenos Aires, Kau, 1940.

JORGE DE LIMA (1895– )

*Poemas,* Rio de Janeiro, A. Noite, 1939; translations by J. Torres Oliveros and C. R. Arechavaleta.

d'Eça, Raul, "Jorge de Lima, gran poeta del Brasil," *Universidad católica bolivariana,* IV (1939), 186-194.

## BRAZILIAN DRAMA IN ENGLISH AND SPANISH TRANSLATIONS

JOSÉ MARTINIANO DE ALENCAR (1829-1877)

"The Jesuit," translated from the Portuguese by Edgardo R. de Britto, *Poetlore,* Boston, XXX (1919), 475-547.

*El guarany,* opera puesta en música por A. Carlos Gomes, Montevideo, 1876.

## BRAZILIAN PROSE FICTION IN ENGLISH AND SPANISH TRANSLATIONS

JOSÉ MARTINIANO DE ALENCAR (1829-1877)

*Iraçéma, the Honey-lips: A Legend of Brazil,* translated with the author's permission by Isabel Burton, London, Bickers, 1886.

*El gaucho: novela brasileña,* versión castellana de E. Amo, Paris, Garnier, [1913].

JOAQUIM MARIA MACHADO DE ASSIS (1839-1908)

*Memorias póstumas de Blas Cubas,* versión castellana de Rafael Mesa López, Paris, Garnier, [1911].

*Memorias póstumas de Blas Cubas,* Buenos Aires, Club del Libro, A.L.A., 1940.

*Don Casmurro,* versión castellana de Rafael Mesa López, Paris, Garnier, [1911].

*Varias historias,* versión española de Rafael Mesa López, Paris, Garnier, [1911].

"Life," translated from the original Portuguese by Isaac Goldberg, *Stratford Journal,* Boston, V (1919), 119-129.

"The Attendant's Confession," "The Fortune-teller," "Life," *Brazilian Tales,* translated from the Portuguese with an introduction by Isaac Goldberg, Boston, The Four Seas Company, 1921.

Verissimo, José, "Machado de Assis," *Revista de América,* Paris, Año 3 (1914), 63-71, 143-154.

ALFREDO D'ESCRAGNOLLE TAUNAY (1843-1899)

*Innocencia: A Story of the Prairie Regions of Brazil,* by Silvio Dinarte [pseud.], London, Chapman and Hall, 1889.

*Inocencia,* Bogotá, Lib. Americana, 1905.

*Inocencia,* Buenos Aires, 1905.

*Inocencia,* Madrid, Pueyo, 1923.

Jones, Maro B., "Introduction," *Innocencia,* Boston, Heath, [1923], xi-xxiii.

EUCLYDES DA CUNHA (1867-1909)

*Los sertones,* traducción del original de Benjamin de Garay, prólogo de Mariano de Vedia, Buenos Aires, [La Imp. Mercatali], 1938 (Biblioteca de autores brasileños traducidos al castellano, 3-4).

ALUIZIO GONÇALVES DE AZEVEDO (1857-1912)

*El mulato,* traducción de Arturo Costa Alvarez, Buenos Aires, 1904 (Biblioteca de "La Nación," 145).

*El mulato,* versión castellana de Jesús de Amber, n.p., 1912.

*A Brazilian Tenement,* translated from the Portuguese by Harry W. Brown, New York, McBride, 1926.

HENRIQUE COELHO NETTO (1864- )

"The Pigeons," *Brazilian Tales,* 121-135. (See above under J. M. Machado de Assis, "The Attendant's Confession.")

*Rey negro,* Buenos Aires, Claridad, 1938.

JOSÉ PEREIRA DA GRAÇA ARANHA (1868-1931)

*Canaán,* Paris, Garnier, n.d.

*Canaan,* translated from the Portuguese by Mariano Joaquin Lorente, with a preface by Guglielmo Ferrero, Boston, The Four Seas Company, 1920.

*Canaán*, traducción y notas de B. Sánchez Sáez, Santiago de Chile, 1935.

"Marta: A Legend of the Celestial Voice," *Inter-America*, English: IV (1920), 95-96.

*El viaje maravilloso*, traducido por Iris B. de Barboza Mello, Buenos Aires, Club del Libro, A.L.A., [1938].

AFRANIO PEIXOTO (1876– )
*La esfinge*, Buenos Aires, 1912.
*La esfinge*, Barcelona, 1920.

JOSÉ BENTO MONTEIRO LOBATO (1883– )
*Urupés*, Buenos Aires, Patria, 1921.
*El comprador de haciendas*, Barcelona, Cervantes, 1923.
*Los ojos que sangran*, Buenos Aires, Tor, 1924.
"Modern Torture," "The Penitent Wag," "The Plantation Buyer," *Brazilian Short Stories*, with an introduction by Isaac Goldberg, Girard, Kansas, Haldeman-Julius, [1925] (Little Blue Book 733).
"The Farm Magnate," *Great Stories of All Nations*, New York, Brentano's, 1927, 926-936.
*El drama de la helada*, Buenos Aires, Edgard, 1929.

PABLO DE OLIVEIRA SETUBAL (1893-1937)
*Domitila: The Romance of an Emperor's Mistress* (*A Marqueza de Santos*), New York, Coward-McCann, 1930.
*La marquesa de Santos*, Buenos Aires, Club del Libro, A.L.A., 1939.

ERICO VERISSIMO (1905– )
*Mirad los lirios del campo*, versión castellana de Matilde de Elía de Etchegoyan, Buenos Aires, Club del Libro, A.L.A., 1940.

LUCIO CARDOSO (1913– )
*Morro de Salgueiro*, Buenos Aires, Claridad, 1939.

JORGE AMADO
*Cacao: la vida de los trabajadores en las fazendas del Brasil*, traducido por Héctor Miri, Buenos Aires, Claridad, 1936.

*Jubiabá,* traducido por Raúl Navarro, Buenos Aires, Imán, 1937.

*Mar muerto,* traducido por Héctor Miri, Buenos Aires, Claridad, 1940.

MARIO DE ANDRADE

*Fräulein,* New York, Macauley, 1933.

GASTÃO CRULS

*Amazonia misteriosa,* Buenos Aires, Claridad, 1938.

HERMAN LIMA

*Garimpos,* Buenos Aires, Claridad, 1939.

MARIO SETTE

*Señora de ingenio,* Buenos Aires, n.d.

# Index of Authors Mentioned in the Outline

Acevedo Díaz, Eduardo, 113
Acuña, Manuel, 58
Agustini, Delmira, 150-151
Alegría, Ciro, 142
Alemán, Mateo, 5
"Almafuerte," 83
Altamirano, Ignacio Manuel, 45, 71-72
Andrade, Olegario Victor, 59-60
Apollinaire, Guillaume, 122
Arciniegas, Ismael Enrique, 83
Arévalo Martínez, Rafael, 146-147, 156
Arguedas, Alcides, 142-143
Ariosto, Ludovico, 2
Arrieta, Rafael Alberto, 155
Ascasubi, Hilario, 46, 61-63, 64
"Ayanque, Simón," 21-22
Azuela, Mariano, 147, 148

Bacon, Francis, Lord, 110
Balbuena, Bernardo de, 17-18
Balzac, Honoré de, 112
Banchs, Enrique, 154
Barletta, Leónidas, 121
Baroja, Pío, 141
Barrios, Eduardo, 139-140
Baudelaire, Charles, 80, 95
Bécquer, Gustavo Adolfo, 81, 95, 96
Bello, Andrés, 30, 35-37
Benavente, Toribio de, 2
Blanco-Fombona, Rufino, 88, 126, 127-128
Blest Gana, Alberto, 70-71
Bolívar, Simón, 31, 34, 41-42
Borges, Jorge Luis, 122, 159
Borja, Francisco de, 5
Boursault, Edmé, 6

Bustamente, Carlos Inga Calixto ("Concolor-corvo"), 23-24
Byron, George Gordon, Lord, 46, 53, 68, 91

Cabeza de Vaca, Álvar Núñez, 7, 13-14
Caesar, Julius, 11
Cambaceres, Eugenio, 72
Campo, Estanislao del, 64-65
Campoamor, Ramón de, 95, 96
Caro, José Eusebio, 57-58
Casal, Julián del, 80, 94
Casas, Bartolomé de las, 2, 14
Castro, Eugenio de, 99
Caviedes, Juan del Valle y, 20-21
Cetina, Gutierre de, 5
Chateaubriand, François René, 46, 69
Chocano, José Santos, 79, 88, 92, 98, 103-104
Cieza de León, Pedro, 2
Coloma, Luis, 84
"Concolorcorvo," 23-24
Contardo, Luis Felipe, 83
Cooper, James Fenimore, 69
Coppée, François, 80
Corneille, Pierre, 6, 26
Cortés, Hernán, 2, 7, 11-12
Cuervo, Rufino José, 36
Cueva, Juan de la, 5

D'Annunzio, Gabriele, 99
Darío, Rubén, 79, 81, 82, 86, 88, 92, 96-99, 100, 101, 102, 109, 156
Delgado, Rafael, 84
Díaz, Leopoldo, 83
Díaz del Castillo, Bernal, 2, 12-13
Díaz Mirón, Salvador, 91-92
Díaz Rodríguez, Manuel, 107, 109, 119

Echeverría, Esteban, 46, 48, **53-54**, 65, 66
Edwards Bello, Joaquín, **141**
Emerson, Ralph Waldo, 110
Ercilla y Zúñiga, Alonso de, 2, **16**, 17
Espronceda, José de, 46, 81
Esquilache, Príncipe de, 5

Fernández de Lizardi, José Joaquín, 29, 30, 42-43
Fiallo, Fabio, 83
Flaubert, Gustave, 96
Flores, Alejandro, 121

Gallego, Juan Nicasio, 29, 34
Gallegos, Rómulo, **144-145**
Gálvez, Manuel, **136-137**
Gamboa, Federico, **111-112**
García Calderón, Francisco, 126, **129**
García Calderón, Ventura, 83, 129
García Lorca, Federico, 122, 126, 160
García Velloso, Enrique, 85
Garcilaso de la Vega, el Inca, **15**
Gautier, Théophile, 80, 90
Godoy Azcayaga, Lucila ("Gabriela Mistral"), **151-152**
Gómez Carillo, Enrique, 83
Gómez de Avellaneda, Gertrudis, **56-57**
Goncourt, Edmond and Jules, 112
Góngora y Argote, Luis de, 6, 11, 22, 91
González de Eslava, Fernán, **24-25**
González Martínez, Enrique, 86, **106**, 119
González Prada, Manuel, 84, 107, **108-109**
Guillén, Nicolas, **157-158**
Güiraldes, Ricardo, **138-139**
Gutiérrez Nájera, Manuel, 80, 82, **90-91**
Gúzmán, Martín Luis, **147-148**

Haya de la Torre, Raúl, 108, 124
Hebreo, León, 15
Heine, Heinrich, 95
Heredia, José María, 30, **37-38**
Heredia, José María de (French), 80, 83
Hernández, José, **65-66**
Hernández, Pero, 13

Herrera y Reissig, Julio, **104-105**
Hidalgo, Bartolomé, **40**
Hojeda, Diego de, 18
Hostos, Eugenio María, **75-76**
Hugo, Victor, 36, 46, 80, 91, 99
Huidobro, Vicente, 122, **158-159**

Ibarbourou, Juana de, **153**
Ibsen, Hendrik, 117
Icaza, Francisco A. de, 83
Icaza, Jorge, **143**
Ingenieros, José, 115
Isaacs, Jorge, 48, **69-70**

Jaimes Freyre, Ricardo, 82, 86, **100-101**
Jiménez, Juan Ramón, 122, 126
Joyce, James, 122, 126
Juana Inés de la Cruz, Sor, 6, **19-20**, 22, 25, 102

Kipling, Rudyard, 133

Lamartine, Alfonse de, 80
Las Casas, Bartolomé de, 2, **14**
Latorre, Mariano, **140**
Leconte de Lisle, Charles, 80, 83
Leguizamón, Martiniano P., **114-115**
Lillo, Baldomero, **116**
López, Luis Carlos, **156-157**
López Albújar, Enrique, **142**
López de Gómara, Francisco, 12
López-Portillo y Rojas, José, 84, **111**
López Velarde, Ramón, **155-156**
López y Fuentes, Gregorio, 148
López y Planes, Vicente, 39
Loveira, Carlos, **145-146**
Luca, Esteban de, **38-39**
Lugones, Leopoldo, 86, **101-102**, 115, 154
Lynch, Benito, **138**

Maeterlinck, Maurice, 80
Magallanes Moure, Manuel, **153-154**
Mallarmé, Stéphane, 80
Mariátegui, José Carlos, 108

Mármol, José, 46, 48, 58, **67-68**
Marroquín, Lorenzo, 84
Martí, José, 80, **92-93**, 97
Martínez de la Rosa, Francisco, 55
Martínez Zuviría, Gustavo ("Hugo Wast"),
   136, **137-138**
Matto de Turner, Clorinda, 84, **113-114**, 142
Mendès, Catulle, 80, 96
Mera, Juan León, **68-69**, 84
"Mistral, Gabriela," **151-152**
Mitre, Bartolomé, **63-64**, 72
Molière, 6
Montaigne, Michel de, 110
Montalvo, Juan, 48, **74-75**, 108
Monteagudo, Bernardo de, 29, **41**
Moreno, Mariano, 29
Musset, Alfred de, 80, 90

Nariño, Antonio, 29, **32**
"Neruda, Pablo," **160**
Nervo, Amado, 82, 86, **102-103**
Núñez, Rafael, 97
Núñez Cabeza de Vaca, Álvar, 7, **13-14**

Obligado, Rafael, **66-67**
Ocantos, Carlos María, 84, **112-113**
Ojeda, Diego de, **18**
Olmedo, José Joaquín, 30, **34-35**, 36
*Ollanta(y)*, **26-27**, 63, 130
Oña, Pedro de, **16-17**
Ortiz, Fernando, 126
Ortiz, José Joaquín, 57
Othón, Manuel José, 83
Oyuela, Calixto, 66

Palacios, Pedro B. ("Almafuerte"), 83
Palés Matos, Luis, 157
Palma, Ricardo, 47, **76-77**
Pardo, Miguel Eduardo, 83
Parra, Teresa de la, **145**
Payró, Roberto J., **115-116**, 117, 118
Peralta Barnuevo, Pedro de, 6, **25-26**
Pereda, José María, 84, 140
Pérez Gáldos, Benito, 75, 83, 84

Peza, Juan de Dios, **59**
Pezoa Velis, Carlos, 83
Picón-Febres, Gonzalo, 83
"Plácido," 45, **54-55**, 66
Poe, Edgar Allan, 95, 133
Prado, Pedro, **140-141**
Proust, Marcel, 122, 126

Quevedo, Francisco Gómez de, **23**
Quintana, Manuel, 29, 34
Quintana Roo, Andrés, **39-40**
Quiroga, Horacio, **133-134**

Rabasa, Emilio, 84
Reyes, Alfonso, 127, **131-132**
Reyes, Neftalí ("Pablo Neruda"), **160**
Reyles, Carlos, 109, **134-135**
Riva Palacio, Vicente, 59
Rivera, José Eustasio, **143-144**, 157
Rodó, José Enrique, 79, 88, 107, **109-110**, 129
Rodríguez Larreta, Enrique, **135-136**
Rojas, Manuel, **141**
Rojas, Ricardo, 126, **129-130**
Romains, Jules, 122
Romero, José Rubén, **149**
Romero García, Vicente, 83
Rousseau, Jean Jacques, 29, 32

Sánchez, Florencio, **117-118**, 121
Sánchez, Luis Alberto, 79, 108, 126
Sarmiento, Domingo Faustino, 36, 48, 63,
   **72-74**, 144
Scarron, Paul, 6
Schiller, Friedrich, 53
Shakespeare, William, 53
Sigüenza y Góngora, Carlos de, 6, **22-23**
Silva, José Asunción, 80, **94-95**
Storni, Alfonsina, **152-153**
Sully-Prudhomme, René, 80

Tablada, José Juan, 83
Tasso, Torquato, 2
Terralla y Landa, Esteban de ("Simón Ayan-
   que"), **21-22**
Torres Bodet, Jaime, **159-160**

Ugarte, Manuel, 79, 88, 126, 128-129
Urbina, Luis G., 83

Valdelomar, Abraham, 142
Valdés, Antonio, 26
Valdés, Gabriel de la Concepción ("Plácido"),
45, 54-55
Valencia, Guillermo, 99-100
Valenzuela, Jesús E., 82, 102
Valera, Juan, 81, 83, 96
Valéry, Paul, 122
Valle y Caviedes, Juan del, 20-21
Varela, Juan Cruz, 52-53
Vasconcelos, José, 126, 130-131

Vasseur, Alvaro Armando, 83
Verlaine, Paul, 80, 81, 90, 97, 99
Viana, Javier de, 132-133

"Wast, Hugo," 136, 137-138
Whitman, Walt, 122, 126
Wilde, Oscar, 99

Xenophon, 11

Zola, Émile, 47, 112, 115, 116
Zorrilla, José, 81
Zorrilla de San Martín, Juan, 60-61